MONEY WITH A PURPOSE

RICK EATON

Trilogy Christian Publishers
A Wholly Owned Subsidiary of Trinity Broadcasting
Network 2442 Michelle Drive Tustin, CA 92780
Copyright © 2018 by Richard L. Eaton
All Scripture quotations, unless otherwise noted, taken from THE HOLY
BIBLE, NEW INTERNATIONAL VERSION®, NIV® Copyright ©
1973, 1978, 1984, 2011 by Biblica, Inc.® Used by permission. All rights
reserved worldwide.
Scripture quotations marked (KJV) taken from The Holy Bible, King
James Version. Cambridge Edition: 1769.
First Trilogy Christian Publishing hardcover edition May 2018
Trilogy Christian Publishing/ TBN and colophon are trademarks of
Trinity Broadcasting Network.
For information about special discounts for bulk purchases, please contact
Trilogy Christian Publishing.
Manufactured in the United States of America
10 9 8 7 6 5 4 3 2 1
Library of Congress Cataloging-in-Publication Data is available.
ISBN 978-1-64088-690-2
ISBN 978-1-64088-691-9 (ebook)

ACKNOWLEDGMENTS

To my amazing wife Robin. There is no way to express the wonderful support you have given me in the writing of this book. Your faith and encouragement on our journey together is behind every letter of every word written here. I have been blessed with a wife that is far beyond what I deserve, and for that I am eternally grateful. I love you more than words can express.

To my two sons, Ryan and Alan, and their wives, Amanda and Lily. You have been so supportive of my heart's desire to communicate what it means to live in a Psalm 112 family. I love you each so much and am thankful God has allowed us to do the Psalm 112 life together. You are each mighty in the Kingdom of God and, because of your hearts for God, your children—Carter, Eli, Mason, and Liam—will also become mighty in the earth.

To Lynn and David White, my sister-in-law and brother-in-law. You are much more than that. We have been the closest of friends and partners for the last 32 years. You have been right in the middle of this venture, reading and re-reading the various drafts of this book and providing invaluable feedback and encouragement. Thank you for being an integral part of this Psalm 112 journey.

To my parents, Herb and Marge Eaton, who showed me what it means to live a lifestyle of generosity. Although in heaven now, their giving hearts live on through the people they impacted. Only my two sisters, Margaret Reichenbecher and Jean Sommerville, can truly appreciate the legacy our parents left us. Our lives are blessed as a result.

To my in-laws, Don and JoAnne Shively, who were instrumental in my Christian growth and development through the years. Although with Jesus now, the love they sowed into my life

i

changed me forever. I would not be where I am today without their prayers and love.

To Joel Sims, my pastor, who took time out of his very busy schedule to read my manuscript and provide excellent suggestions and comments. You have been a great pastor to my family and me, filling us weekly with the anointed word of God. Thank you.

To two amazing missionary couples, Ellie and Rodney Hein and Ginger and Rob Carman, who have laid their lives down for the sake of the gospel and have been a tremendous source of inspiration in my life. Only God knows the lives that have been changed as a result of your ministries. I am honored to call you my friends.

To Tripp Douglas, my nephew, who used his outstanding talents to design this book's cover and has encouraged me in its publication. Your Psalm 112 heart is affecting the world for good.

To a wonderful group of family members with whom I work. To Amanda Douglas, Reagan and Jason Peets, Gene Gardner, and Grant Gardner. You make working with family fun and easy. Our work together is changing lives for the kingdom. And to the rest of our Mississippi family, Kim Gardner, Tracey Gardner, Brad and Tia Gardner, Ashleigh Gardner, Jo White, and John White, thanks for being such an important part of my life.

To our business partner, Johnny Morgan, who demonstrates his generosity in a quiet and unassuming manner and has changed the lives of multitudes in Mississippi for good. You are a good man.

Finally, this book would never have been written without the word of the Lord delivered to me by God's faithful servant Patti Alex, who told me over 30 years ago that I was a Psalm 112 man and started me on this great journey. Thank you, Heavenly

Acknowledgments

Father for making your good will known to us and for taking us from glory to glory as we behold you. Your goodness endures continually!

MONEY WITH A PURPOSE

TABLE OF CONTENTS

PROLOGUE
MY PSALM 112 STORY

You're a Psalm 112 Man!

Nearly 32 years ago, as I was standing at the back of our church sanctuary waiting for the 10:00 am service to begin, a woman in our church in Flowood, Mississippi greeted me with a simple statement that led to a revolution in my life. She said, "Rick, you're a Psalm 112 Man!" Unsure of the correct response to a greeting like that, I simply said, "Thank you." At the time, I had no idea what Psalm 112 said and certainly did not understand the impact these simple words would have on my life over the next 30-plus years. Ordinarily, this was the kind of thing that I could have immediately dismissed or joked about. However, because I had great respect for the spiritual maturity in this woman's life, and I knew she would not make statements like this without good reason, I thought about what she said. These were not idle words that someone uses when there is nothing else to say. This was not small talk. There was something deep and powerful contained in those words. My reaction was a little like Mary's when the shepherds told her what the angel of the Lord had said to them about Jesus. Luke 2:19 says, "She pondered these things in her heart." So did I.

Like many things we may hear over the course of a lifetime, the words spoken to me, in and of themselves, were nothing that anyone would consider life-changing. Most, I'm sure, would have moved on from that exchange and never had a second thought about it. There was something about those words, however, and the manner in which they were delivered that caused the message to lodge in my heart. With my interest piqued, I opened my Bible to Psalm 112 and began to read. I have to say, this particular psalm interested me a great deal because it described the attributes of a man who feared the Lord and delighted greatly in His commandments. What

I read sounded awesome, but it did not sound much like a description of me at that time in my life. This woman, however, had just said that I was a Psalm 112 Man. As I thought about this statement and began to read the contents of Psalm 112, something began to happen on the inside of me. Hope began to build in me. The words of Psalm 112, although penned over 3000 years ago, was God himself telling me how He saw me.

Praise ye the Lord! Blessed is the man who fears the Lord, who delights greatly in His commandments. His seed shall be mighty upon earth; the generation of the upright shall be blessed. Wealth and riches shall be in his house and his righteousness endures forever. Unto the upright there arises light in the darkness; he is gracious and full of compassion and righteous. A good man shows favor and lends; he will guide his affairs with discretion. Surely he shall not be moved forever; the righteous shall be in everlasting remembrance. He shall not be afraid of evil tidings; his heart is fixed, trusting in the Lord. His heart is established, he shall not be afraid, until he sees his desire upon his enemies. He hath disbursed, he has given to the poor; his righteousness endures forever; his horn will be exalted with honor. The wicked will see it and be grieved; he shall gnash with his teeth and melt away; the desire of the wicked shall perish. (Psalm 112 NKJV)

Wow!!! Could that possibly be me? Sure, I was a believer. I loved God. I delighted in the things of God. However, what I was reading did not exactly resemble the guy in the mirror. It wasn't that I didn't want to be like the guy described in Psalm 112, it's just the reality of my life at that point did not look like what I was reading in this psalm. Don't misunderstand, I was certainly blessed. I had a great wife and a great son. (I now have two great sons, two great daughters-in-law, and four grandchildren.) I had a good business, a good church, and a good life. I just seemed to be missing a few key components like wealth and riches; like being able to show favor and lend; like not being afraid of bad news...like disbursing abroad and taking care of the needs of the poor. But…the seed had been planted. Hope had been ignited. The word had been planted in good soil and was beginning to take hold.

In retrospect, God's word to me through the lady in my church was similar to the word Gideon received from the angel of the Lord as he hid in the winepress from the Midianites. In Judges 6:12, the angel of the Lord appeared to Gideon and said, "The Lord is with you, you mighty man of valor." The angel who spoke for God told him he was a mighty man of valor while he was hiding in fear of the Midianites!

I can just picture Gideon's reaction when the angel called him a mighty man of valor. He probably looked over his shoulder to see if there was someone behind him who was the intended recipient of this greeting. What Gideon probably did not understand was that God likes "to call those things that be not as though they are."

God sees us as we can be, not as we are now!

I have to give you a little background that will help you understand why this psalm became such a transforming word in my life. At the time, even though I was a Bible-believing Christian, I had a real problem with the "prosperity message" that was being taught in many Charismatic and Word churches. As with many good and scripturally supportable doctrines that find their way into the church, the prosperity message was miscommunicated by some and misunderstood by many others as a way to get God to make you rich. I got so offended by the excesses and mis-focus of this teaching, that I missed the important truth of this message. I went into the ditch on the other side of the road as far as this doctrine was concerned and developed the mistaken notion that you could not be rich and a faithful follower of Christ at the same time. I thought you had to be poor to be spiritual. What a stupid idea that was!

A pastor of mine used to say, "Faith begins where the will of

God is known." In other words, you cannot have faith for something until you know it is God's will for you to have it. We find God's will in his word. The word given to me from Psalm 112, coupled with the word from my pastor about faith beginning where God's will is known, pulled me out of the ditch I was in and helped me begin to renew my mind based on what the Bible actually said about my life.

As I write this, I am 62 years old. It has been 32 years since the day I first heard those words, "Rick, you are a Psalm 112 Man!" As I look back over the last thirty-two years since those words were spoken to me, I can see how God has made the truth of Psalm 112 a reality in my life. Have I arrived? Certainly not! Is there more? Absolutely! As the Apostle Paul said, "I am pressing toward the mark for the prize of the high calling of God in Christ Jesus." I will never stop pressing and believing God for more until the day Jesus returns or I finish my course on earth. That is what a Psalm 112 Man does!

I actually began assembling notes for this book over ten years ago. As time has passed, and as I have continued to meditate on this psalm, as well as other scripture from the Bible, new revelation of the application of this psalm continues to find root in my heart. This does not surprise me since Hebrews 4:12 tells us, "For the word of God is alive and active. Sharper than any double-edged sword, it penetrates even to the dividing of soul and spirit, joints and marrow; it judges the thoughts and attitudes of the heart." The word is alive! It continues to find ways to come alive in our hearts and lives and to mold our thinking and transform us into people who are alive each day to the purposes of God.

One of those "new revelations" is that this psalm applies not only to individuals, but also to families. This understanding has become clearer to me over the last 20 years as I have worked alongside my brother-in-law who has also been transformed by Psalm 112. Not only have we become best friends whose families spend a lot of time together, we have also worked together in unity with our wives, children, and in-laws to see God take a normally mundane business operation and turn it into a thriving place of purpose that is making an impact around the world. As a result, Psalm 112:2 is being fulfilled before our eyes, "his descendants will be mighty in the earth."

Maybe you want to be a Psalm 112 Man too. Well, let me tell you that every promise in the word is "Yes and Amen" to those who will take hold of it by faith. Am I special? Yes, but no more special than you! If you are a believer, you too can be a Psalm 112 Man (or woman).

This book is written to tell you what I have learned over the last thirty-two years about the truth contained in Psalm 112. Actually, you will find the truth of Psalm 112 repeated throughout the word of God if you look for it. This book is designed to spur you on to becoming all that God has called you to be in your home, in your church, in business, and in your community. My goal in writing this short book is to impact your thinking and to change your perspective. "For as a man thinks in his heart, so is he" (Proverbs 23:7 KJV). The secret to changing your situation in life is to begin to think differently. What we think about and mediate on determines how we act. Our actions set in motion our course in life. The course we take in life determines the impact we make. So my goal is to change your perspective and thinking to that of a Psalm 112 Man.

So how do you become a Psalm 112 Man? First by seeing the truth that God wants you to be the kind of person described in this psalm and secondly, by becoming a doer of the principles laid out in this great psalm. The benefits that are described in this psalm will be a by-product of the actions of the man (or woman) who applies the principles. If you want to become a Psalm 112 Man, receive what you read in the pages of this book, act on them, and believe that you too are a Psalm 112 Man!

As we take a closer look at Psalm 112, I will use the New International Version of the Bible because I think it gives us a little better insight into the meaning of this psalm. This is to take nothing away from the power contained in the King James Version. In fact, as I memorized and have meditated on this psalm, I have always done so using the King James Version. Regardless of which translation you prefer, these Spirit-inspired words can change your life.

Because there is significant truth to be found in every one of the 10 verses of this chapter, I have devoted a chapter to each verse. My prayer is that Psalm 112 becomes a reality in your life and that you and your household experience the joy that living as a Psalm 112 family brings.

CHAPTER 1

THE RECIPE FOR HAPPINESS

Verse 1 – Praise the Lord. Blessed is the man who fears the Lord, who finds great delight in His commands.

The movie Field of Dreams was released back in 1989. That was thirty-one years ago, yet, every time I am flipping through the channels and discover that the movie is on, I stop and watch. My wife laughs at me when I do this and usually says, "Oh, no, Field of Dreams! Are you going to watch it again?", which really means, "Am I going to have to go do something else?" She enjoyed watching it with me the first few times, but then she had seen it enough. Eventually, she bought me the DVD that I could watch by myself anytime I wanted without interrupting our TV time together.

I think the thing that draws me to that movie is all the great lines. One such line near the end of the movie is when John Kinsella and his son Ray are discussing whether the Iowa corn fields, where Ray has built a baseball field, is heaven. Ray asks his father if there is a heaven, and his response is, "Oh yeah. It's the place where dreams come true."

Actually dreams come true when we fear the Lord and make His word our delight. Dreams come true in the life of the man or woman whose heart is after God. Dreams come true in the center of God's will!

The Hebrew word translated "Praise the Lord" is Hallelu Yah. The truth that the psalmist is about to reveal to us in the following verses is preceded by giving praise to God for His great statutes and precepts that endure to all generations. Like the Psalmist, I am awestruck by the certainty and power contained in the truth of God's word. Thank God that in this constantly changing world, there is something in our lives that will never change…the truth of God's word. When all else fails, His word will remain. Heaven and earth may pass away, but His words will never pass away. Regardless of what the experts may say, it is the word of God that should be the final authority in a believer's life. We can trust the word of God!

Blessed is the man. The Hebrew word esher can also be translated "happy." Happy is the man who fears the Lord. What does it mean to fear the Lord? In this sense, to "fear the Lord" means to revere Him, to be in awe of His greatness, and to esteem highly His every word. It means to place great importance on everything he says because we recognize the greatness of the one from whom these words emanate.

There used to be an old stock brokerage and consulting firm named E.F. Hutton. Years ago, they had a television commercial that put them on the map in terms of name recognition. There were many versions of the commercial, but all contained a couple of people talking with a crowd around them and one person says to the other, "Well, E.F. Hutton says…" At these words the crowd around them stops what they are doing and leans in to hear what E.F. Hutton's advice would be. The narrator then said, "When E.F. Hutton speaks, people listen." The point was, advice that came from the E.F. Hutton stock brokerage and consulting firm was highly sought after by the multitudes and that those who heeded the words of E.F. Hutton would benefit.

E.F. Hutton has come and gone, but the words of their catchy commercial still provide us with wisdom we can apply in hearing God's word. When God speaks, the wise man will listen. The man who has learned to reverence and esteem highly his creator and the words that proceed from his mouth is a happy man. This reverence is evidenced by the fact that this man takes great delight in hearing God's precepts and is receptive to hearing the truth of His word. This man recognizes the divine power and life that comes from the words spoken by God. This man would rather hear what God has to say on the matter than hear the opinions of the world's greatest minds. This man recognizes that God's word is the final authority in any matter, and only His words bring life and peace.

The words of God are not just idle words. Each syllable of a word from God contains within itself the ability to create and transform. Hebrews 11:3 tells us, "By faith we understand that the universe was formed at God's command, so that what is seen was not made out of what was visible." Do you need some things created or transformed in your life? Then the word of God is the place to begin. The man who recognizes the authority and finality of the words spoken by God is indeed a happy and blessed man.

"Happy is the man who reveres His creator and has made the word of God the foundational authority in his life"(Psalm 112:1, author's paraphrase).

We find the following in Colossians 1:16-17. "For in him all things were created: things in heaven and on earth, visible and invisible, whether thrones or powers or rulers or authorities; all things were created through him and for him. He is before all things, and in him all things hold together."

In order to find happiness in life, we have to begin by

recognizing God's authority in our lives. In Him, all things hold together. Outside of Him, things begin to unravel, or, as we say in Mississippi, "The wheels begin to come off." Living life without God in the center is a recipe for unhappiness. However, making Jesus your Lord and determining to live your life in accordance with His commands is the beginning of your happiest days.

We are given numerous examples in the Old Testament of men who decided for a season that they had a better plan than God. Take a look at the life of Jacob, who later was renamed Israel. God spoke to Jacob in Bethel when he was escaping for his life in fear that his brother Esau was going to kill him. In Genesis 28, God made a covenant promise to Jacob that he would protect him and prosper him and bring him safely back to that land (Bethel). Jacob worked for twenty years for his uncle Laban in Paddan Aram. During this time, despite being cheated and taken advantage of by his uncle, Jacob prospered greatly. Then one night in a dream, God told Jacob to return to Bethel, the land of his fathers (the place where God had made a promise to Jacob twenty years earlier). Jacob began his journey and saw God protect him along the way from an angry uncle and from his brother Esau. However, rather than returning to Bethel as God had instructed him, Jacob decided to buy land and settle in Shechem. He did not value the words of God above everything else. He thought his plan was better, so he did his own thing. As many of us have experienced in our lives, if we exclude God from our plans, the fabric begins to unravel, and the wheels begin to come off. Well, the wheels came off for Jacob in Shechem. His daughter was raped and two of his sons attacked and murdered all the men of Shechem. Now it appears to Jacob that the covenant promise of God is over. The people in the surrounding lands are going to hear about what he and his sons have done. He will be hated and despised, and his life will once again be in danger. Wisely however, Jacob then makes the decision to return to the place of God's promise, Bethel.

If we are honest about it, we too have had times when we decided our way was best. Unfortunately, when we step outside God's idea for us, things can unravel quickly. If there is a lesson to be learned from Jacob's mistake, it is that he should have esteemed the word spoken to him by God and acted on the words, "Return to Bethel." He should have returned immediately to Bethel rather than settling in Shechem. God's instructions are not intended to harm us. They are intended to bring us to the bright future he has in store for us. Whenever we are faced with choices in life, our decisions should always be based upon what God says first. If our ways and desires run contrary to what God says in his word, we need to adjust our thinking and our choices to His ways. It will always turn out better for us when we follow after the ways God has ordained. This is what it means to "fear the Lord" and to "delight in his commands." When faced with the choice of doing it our way or God's way, the Psalm 112 Man chooses God's way. As a result, the Psalm 112 Man is blessed (happy)!

Let me give you an easy example of doing life God's way versus our way. One way that we believers prove God's provision for us is in the tithe. We bring the first tenth of our increase into His storehouse, the local church, as an act of faith in God's provision. We then believe that God will bless the remaining 90%. Malachi 3:8-12 gives us a picture of the importance of bringing our tithe into the storehouse first. When we do this, we can expect God to open the windows of heaven and pour out a blessing that contains so much, we won't have room enough to receive it all.

However, if we make the choice to spend the first 10% on ourselves and give to God out of whatever is left (if any), we are shutting ourselves off from the open windows of heaven. It's our choice, but the Psalm 112 Man chooses wisely because he greatly values the word of God and knows that God is only thinking of our good and our benefit. Doing his precepts will not cause us harm. Delighting in his word brings great happiness.

Happy is the man who finds great delight in God's words.

CHAPTER 2

RAISING MIGHTY CHILDREN

Verse 2 - His children will be mighty in the land. Each generation of the upright will be blessed.

I can identify with the Apostle John when he said, "I have no greater joy than to hear that my children are walking in the truth" (3 John 4). To see our children grow and make good Bible-based choices and begin to apply God-established precepts and principles in their own lives really does bring great joy and satisfaction in our hearts. In many ways it is a relief to see this happening because we know that by building their own house on a solid rock, our children are protecting themselves from the destructive forces of life that can wreak havoc in the lives of those who have built on inferior foundations. By building on the solid foundation of God's word, our children are also planting seeds of greatness in their lives. These seeds will produce a harvest of righteousness that will impact their generation for good, and they will accomplish amazing exploits for the Kingdom of God.

The Hebrew word for "mighty" in this verse is gibbor and can be translated as powerful, champion, chief, mighty one, strong man, or valiant man. It is the same word used to describe

Gideon in Judges 6:12. It is also the same word that is used to describe King David's 37 Mighty Men (II Samuel 23:8-39 and I Chronicles 11:10-47) that were part of his army and were responsible for winning great battles against the enemies of God. They brought the nation of Israel into great prominence under David's rule. These were men like Jashobeam who was famous for slaying 800 of the enemy at one time. Then there was Eleazar, who, along with David, stood his ground against the Philistines when the men of Israel had retreated. He fought until his hand was stuck to the sword and achieved a great victory. There was also Shammah, who alone defended a field of lentils against a Philistine attack, and the Lord brought a great victory there. This list includes Benaiah who was famous for killing two Moabite heroes and an Egyptian man that was 7 ½ feet tall. Benaiah also jumped into a pit on a snowy day to kill a lion.

These men all had one thing in common, they believed that David was the anointed King of Israel according to word of the Lord concerning Israel (I Chronicles 11:10 NKJV). They esteemed the word of the Lord highly and acted accordingly. As a result, these men were strong and mighty in the land, and they did great exploits. Honoring God's word is what makes our children mighty in the land as well. Everything else is secondary. And the result will be that our children will be mighty and strong and will do great exploits.

Why is it that the children of the man that highly esteems God's word will be mighty in the land? Do you remember why God chose to establish his covenant through Abraham? "For I know him, that he will command his children and his household after him, and they shall keep the way of the LORD, to do justice and judgment; that the LORD may bring upon Abraham that which He hath spoken of him" (Genesis 18:19 KJV).

The things that Abraham had learned from God and his faith

in what God had said would be taught to his children. He did this through both teaching and training. Abraham was called the Father of Faith because he simply believed what God told him. He esteemed His word greatly. It is this faith and trust in God and His word that Abraham would communicate to his children and grandchildren. And as this faith and trust in God and his word was developed in Abraham's descendants, they would become mighty in the earth as Abraham had.

Proverbs 22:6 (NKJV) tells us to "Train up a child in the way he should go and when he is old, he will not depart from it." Children are trained not only through hearing our words of instruction but also by observing our lives. And as the old adage says, "There is more caught than taught." Our example carries more weight than our words. Abraham's children knew that he believed God. He told them about his faith, but he also showed them his faith. They knew he highly esteemed the words spoken to him by God, and they saw the result and the blessing that came on his life because of his faith in God. Our children see it too.

I can remember growing up in my parent's household and seeing my father give financial gifts to people in our church who needed it when he thought no one was looking. Although others may not have seen it, his son sure did, and it made a lasting impact on my life.

I had an opportunity to visit with my father in the hospital a few weeks before he passed away, and I asked him about the secret to his success in his life. My dad was a very smart man who had been trained in electrical engineering. He worked in that area most of his life and became an officer and shareholder in a highly successful company that manufactured electrical equipment for the mining industry. His response to me was, "Always give the first of every dollar to the church (the tithe), put some of every dollar earned aside for savings/investment, and live within your means (spend less than you make)." Of course, living within your means meant that there would be money left over to help others when they needed help. By the time I asked my Dad this question, I already knew what his answer would be. I was now grown and had children of my own. I knew what his answer would be because he lived these three principles out in front of me. I learned these precepts by the example of his life. As a result of the application of these principles, I believe our family has been spared many of the financial hardships that people face who do not apply these principles. Could my Dad have taught me these principles by telling me what the word says? Of course! However, I learned them by watching him.

One of the things he loved to do was help people with their education costs. I think this was important to him because when he was a young man, a wealthy business owner took interest in my father and helped him with his education costs. My father had lost his dad when he was a young boy, and he suddenly was forced into the "man of the family" role. He helped his mother provide for his two sisters and brother. So the educational help from the wealthy business owner was an important component of his success. He never forgot that kindness extended to him, and I saw it repeated through his generosity time and time again in his life. When my father finally retired from the board of the company on which he served many years, the company established an engineering scholarship in his name that would fund college educations for many deserving students over the years. It was quite a tribute to my dad, whose heart was to help others like he had been helped.

This kind of giving heart cannot be obtained only by hearing the precepts taught. You receive a heart to give by observing the example of such a heart in action. More is caught than taught. Our children need to see us acting on the word of God. They need to see us living out our faith. This is what training is all about. It is what will stay with them when they are old.

When our two boys were young, I decided that we needed to locate some needy families to help at Christmastime. Our children had never really been exposed to the poverty that was the life that many in our city lived every day. Our church had operated programs that adopted specific needy families at certain times of the year, but our family's involvement had been tangential at best. We would bring food or clothing to the church which was then distributed by someone else to those in need. It was time for that to change! My kids were going to see what poverty looked like and see that there were real people suffering in neighborhoods that were only a short, fifteen-minute drive from where we lived. It was not far in proximity, but it was a world away.

We loaded up the car with some new toys that Robin had wrapped for us along with a couple of turkeys and some canned goods that could be used to prepare a Christmas meal. We set off for the western part of our city to deliver the goods to recipients that we would select as we drove through the area. As we drove past Gun Street (the literal name of the street) and Prosperity Street (an oxymoron if there ever was one), we soon discovered the reason why most people did their giving of this sort through pre-established church or local mission programs. How would we find the right person? How could we determine whether those we selected were truly in need? And most importantly, how would I navigate the streets of these rough neighborhoods with two boys, a few presents, a couple of turkeys and some canned goods, without exposing ourselves to the criminal element of this area of town?

The consensus of our group was that we should avoid Gun Street because there was probably a good reason it was given that name. We would leave Gun Street to the professionals who knew what they were doing. Within a few blocks of Gun Street, we discovered Prosperity Street. Prosperity Street appeared to be anything but prosperous, but we decided the residents of the street might be applying the Biblical principle of "calling those things that be not as though they were", and it would be a safe enough place to make our deliveries.

As we made our way down Prosperity Street, we attracted the stares of kids and adults that were curious about this vehicle that they did not recognize driving slowly through their neighborhood. They probably thought the car could be filled with drug dealers looking for a place to do their deal or gang members looking for a drive-by shooting victim. Undoubtedly, their concerns were relieved when we drove close enough for the curious onlookers to see that the occupants of this unknown car were harmless, wannabe do-gooders that were a little out of their element. We finally spotted a couple of ladies with their children walking along the sidewalk in front of what were presumably their houses. We had prayed that God would lead us to the right people to bless with the food and presents. And since we were anxious to complete our mission and get out of Dodge, we decided that God had led us to these people and that they should be the recipients of out gifts.

We rolled down the car window as we slowly approached the ladies who were obviously suspect of our intentions and asked them if they would like the fixings for a Christmas dinner and a few presents for the kids. Although reluctant to believe that someone would just drive by offering gifts without condition or obligation on their part, they agreed, and we began unloading the car and filling the arms of the women and children that were there, with neighbors looking on in fascination. We left the car running as we passed out the gifts and were gone within 60 seconds. We arrived home about 15 minutes later with my two sons having been on their first, although brief, "Mission

Trip."

Although this ill-conceived attempt to expose our children to the needs of others happened about 24 years ago, my oldest son still remembers the event like it happened yesterday. This mission trip was probably not the main reason, but both sons have grown into men who have hearts for God and others. I have witnessed both sons stepping out in acts of generosity to meet the needs of others and being the hands and feet of Jesus extended just like we did on Prosperity Street many years before. It is vitally important that our children be exposed to the needs of the world around them and to be shown ways that they can participate in changing their world for the better. They need to know that their lives have purpose and that their purpose is always intended to impact others for good.

Robin and I have maintained close friendships with numerous missionaries, pastors, and evangelists through the years whose faith in God and His word have been evident in their extraordinary lives. Because we fellowshipped often with these amazing people, our children also had opportunities to be exposed to these heroes of faith, listening to their stories and seeing their faith in action. This also made a great impact on our children and, I'm sure, contributed to their desire to live for God and see the word of God come alive in their own lives. It also has exposed them to opportunities to get involved in the lives of people around the world through their giving.

In 2008, Robin and I, along with Robin's sister, Lynn, and her husband, David, formed a not-for-profit foundation to use in our missions giving. Over the last 10 years, the four of us have involved our children and their spouses in the foundation and its activities. They are now participating with us in making the decisions about which projects the foundation adopts. We all have mission projects that are near to our hearts and that we want to be involved with financially. We are doing our best to pass the operational baton of the foundation to the next generation. As our children's children grow, our hope is that our grandchildren will follow in the footsteps of their parents and grandparents and will see the importance of making a positive impact on their generation through their giving. For our grandchildren to follow in our footsteps, they will need to see how important the foundation's giving is to us and to their parents. They will be trained in setting goals for the foundation, they will establish relationships with missionaries the foundation supports, and they will discover their own opportunities to do good with the resources God has given them.

THE FATHER'S ROLE

This is probably the appropriate time to take a rabbit trail that has direct bearing on verse 2, "His children shall be mighty in the earth." As important as the mother is in any home in ensuring the stability and well-being of a family, the father's role in seeing his children become "mighty in the land" is paramount. Everyone loves their mother. Our mothers love us no matter what we do. We ran to our mothers when we skinned our knees as kids. We confided in our mothers when our relationships weren't going like we wanted. Our mothers were our chief confidants and counselors and were our biggest cheerleaders and supporters. However, based on a host of statistical surveys conducted over the last 25 years, the truth is our fathers have a greater impact than our mothers on whether or not we follow after God. And consequently, they are a huge factor in determining whether their children become "mighty in the land."

There have been numerous studies on the issue of a father's influence on his children's decisions about "religion" and specifically about whether the children become Christians or church attenders. A study performed in 1994 by Swiss researchers Werner Haug and Phillipe Warner found that a father's regular church attendance was by far the most important factor in determining whether his children grew up to be church attenders. The mother's church attendance had a very small influence on the children's decision to attend church. If the father was a regular church attender, 66-75% of children became church attenders whether their mothers attended church or not. If the father was not a regular church attender, less than 25% of the children became church attenders, even if their mothers attended regularly.

Fathers, how we live our lives for God plays an extremely important part in seeing Psalm 112:2 fulfilled in their lives. The reason our children are mighty in the land is because we have taught them by instruction and by example to love God and his word. They have seen a Psalm 112 Man in action. Because of that, they become Psalm 112 people as well.

I was blessed to have a father that lived a life in front of me that was an example of what living a life for God looked like. A lot of what I have become is a result of seeing my father live his life with God as his priority. What about those, however, who did not have a father who loved God or grew up without a father at all? Well, verse two has you covered. The last part of verse two tells us, "The generation of the upright will be blessed." The upright are those who are in good standing with God. They are those whose hearts are right before God. They are those who love God and His word that are described in verse 1. So regardless of whether or not you had a father who esteemed God highly, you can do it. You can have a godly line that begins with you! Your children can be mighty in the land because of the choice you make to love and serve God.

The Hebrew word translated "blessed" in verse 2 is not the same word that is translated as blessed in verse 1. In verse 1, the Hebrew word is "eser" and can be translated "happy."

The Hebrew word in verse 2 is "barak" and can be translated "praise", "salute" or, "congratulate." We "barak" God when we praise him and acknowledge all the great things he has done. However, verse 2 says the upright will be "barak." The upright will be praised, congratulated and saluted. So, does this mean that God praises us? Does God salute us?

Do you remember the verse in Matthew 6:6 that says, "But when you pray, go into your room, close the door and pray to your Father, who is unseen. Then your Father, who sees what is done in secret will reward you."

This sounds to me like God saluting us, congratulating us, and praising us for what we do in secret. God, however, rewards us openly! The generation of the upright will be praised, saluted, and congratulated by God for choosing to fear Him and taking great delight in His word.

Matthew 25:23 gives us another example of the Master showing barak or praise to his servant. "His master replied, 'Well done, good and faithful servant! You have been faithful with a few things; I will put you in charge of many things. Come and share your master's happiness!' I would much rather have the praise of God than the praise of men. The praise of God comes with great reward.

Can you picture your sons and daughters standing before God in heaven and hearing these words spoken to them? "Well Done!." Can you imagine the joy that would fill your heart to hear the Master say these words to your children? What a great conclusion to the life of a Psalm 112 Man!

His children will be mighty in the land. Each generation of the upright will be blessed (Psalm 112:2).

CHAPTER 3

WEALTHY AND RIGHTEOUS

Verse 3 – Wealth and riches will be in their houses, and their righteousness endures forever.

When I first read Psalm 112, I have to admit that it was verse 3 that caught my attention. I had just been called a "Psalm 112 Man" by this well-respected lady in our church. If what she said was true, then I was being called a wealthy man! To be totally transparent, I stopped reading at this verse and began to let this concept sink in. Could this really be true? Did God really see me as wealthy, and was he OK with this?

You have to understand my thinking about wealth, riches, and righteousness at this point in my life to fully grasp the impact this one verse made on me. I had been turned off by the prosperity message that had been preached in some circles during the 1980s. The message that God wants you to be rich seemed selfish to me. It seemed to focus on improving one's own lifestyle and comfort rather than being a disciple of Christ and being led by the Spirit. When I compared the message that "God wants you rich" to the example of someone like

Mother Teresa, the Catholic sister who ministered to the lowest of the low in Calcutta, India, I felt the two could not have been more diametrically opposed. One message was all about "giving" and the other was all about "getting." On one hand, I saw missionaries whom I respected greatly, giving everything they had for the sake of the gospel. And on the other hand, I heard preachers telling us God wanted us to live in bigger houses and drive nicer cars. This apparent contradiction in what God wanted for his people drove me to the conclusion that you could not be wealthy and righteous at the same time. Wealth and righteousness were at opposite ends of the spectrum in my thinking. They were two lifestyles that could not co-exist. I thought if you were truly spiritual, then wealth would not be in the picture. My basis for this thought was the story of the rich young ruler whom Jesus told to give it all away to satisfy the one thing he lacked.

This philosophy that I had developed, however, did not keep me from pursuing wealth. Like most Americans, I worked at growing my business to generate profits so I could improve my lifestyle. I wanted to have an abundance so I could live a better life, provide a comfortable lifestyle for my family, and be a generous giver. However, in the back of my mind, I had this mistaken idea that if I was going to live for God, there was a limit to the amount of money I could make. I remember sitting on the beach while on a family vacation in the mid 1980s and praying this prayer, "Father if you will allow me to make $50,000 a year, I will never need anything more." That was a stupid prayer that was prayed in ignorance, and I am sure that my Heavenly Father was on his throne in heaven shaking his head in disbelief. He probably turned to Jesus and said, "We won't be answering that prayer. He will come around soon and realize that is not Our will."

My thinking about wealth and riches had driven me off the path of God's will and taken me into the ditch on the side of the road. I was a little like Saul on the road to Damascus when Jesus told him, "It is hard for you to kick against the goads." Life outside of God's will is hard and difficult, but the yoke of God's will is easy and light. My wrong thinking about the will of God concerning wealth and riches was making life difficult for me. "But, the path of the just is as the shining light that shines brighter and brighter until the full light of day" (Proverbs 4:18 NKJV). Thankfully, God had mercy on me and brought someone into my life to bring light to my path. I had strayed off that path by my misguided thinking and by allowing my beliefs to be shaped by what I saw and heard rather than by what the word of God said. Psalm 119:105 tells us, "Your word is a lamp for my feet, a light on my path." It is the word of God that keeps us in the center of His will, and it is His word alone that gives light and life.

Mel Piper was my pastor for a short time in the mid 1980s. He went home to be with the Lord a number of years ago, but he used to say, "Faith begins where the will of God is known." I don't think this quote was original with Mel, but I give him credit for it because I heard it first from him. This statement was instrumental in the shift in my thinking about wealth and riches. Until you know that it is God's will for you to have something in your life, whether it is healing, provision, peace, a good marriage, etc. you can't really have the faith to believe for that thing. Until I received the light of God's word about wealth and riches contained in Psalm 112, I had no faith to receive it.

When I read verse 3 of Psalm 112, a spark of hope was ignited in my heart. Hope is the expectation of something good on the horizon. It is not faith, but it is the beginning of faith. It is the place where faith begins. Hebrews 11 tells us that faith is the substance of things hoped for. In other words, faith is born out of hope. The word of God gives us hope on which our faith is built.

This verse was such a life-changing revelation to me because it told me that I could be wealthy and righteous at the same time. The wealth and riches of the Psalm 112 Man do not lead him away from God. His righteousness (right standing with God) endures, remains, and stands tall. You did not have to disavow one to have the other! It wasn't a matter of wealth or righteousness; we can experience wealth and righteousness at the same time.

This one word from God changed everything. The battle between wealth and righteousness that had been raging on the inside of me was dissolved immediately when the light of God's word shone on it. I realized the will of God provided for both wealth and righteousness, and they were not mutually exclusive lifestyles. My argument had been based on what I had observed others say and do and not on what God had said. God said it, and as far as I was concerned, that settled it. You could, in fact, be wealthy and righteous at the same time!

Although my thinking had been corrected, I still had no idea what a wealthy and righteous lifestyle would look like. But the important part had been settled. I knew God's will and I would begin to believe that God would make me the kind of man that Psalm 112 described. I liked the sound of that, "Wealth and riches will be in his house and his righteousness endures forever."

I began to make Psalm 112:3 part of my daily prayer and confession about myself and my family. I even combined multiple scriptures together that formed somewhat of a montage of scriptural declarations. One of my favorites was, "There's wealth in my house, and I love my spouse." This came from combining Psalm 112:3 with Ephesians 5:25 ("Husbands love your wives as Christ loved the church"). Whatever combination was used, Psalm 112:3 became a part of my daily declaration routine. I highly recommend doing this with any scripture you may be standing on in faith for its fulfillment in your life. It brings faith to your heart (faith comes by continuously hearing the word of God), and it keeps what you are believing God for at the forefront of your thoughts.

A few years ago, I received a gift from one of my sons and his family for Father's Day. My family knows how important Psalm 112 is to me (and now to them), and they knew about my daily declarations about being a Psalm 112 Man. So they gave me a large clay tile engraved with the words of Psalm 112. I have that clay tile displayed in my office where I see it daily, reminding me that God still sees me as a Psalm 112 Man and that this is the life to which we are called.

WEALTH AND RICHES

Notice that verse 3 says "Wealth and riches will be in their houses." Is there a difference between wealth and riches? As a matter of fact there is! Two different Hebrew words are used in this verse that are translated as wealth and riches. At first glance you might think that they are the same (wealth means riches and riches means wealth). However, there is far more to these two words than that. The Hebrew word translated riches is ser and is correctly translated as "riches" or "accumulated riches". The Hebrew word translated wealth is hon and can be translated as "substance", "enough", or "wealth." If you dig a little deeper into the origins of this word however, you will find that the word is connected with another Hebrew word, on, which means "generative power" or "strength". Hon actually means substance that has the ability to generate more substance or riches. The wealth that is in our houses has the ability to increase and multiply and produce more. Wealth carries with it the ability to produce riches. In other words, wealth produces riches. My translation is, "Wealth and its generative power will be in and produce accumulated riches in their houses and their righteousness endures forever"(Psalm 112:3, author's paraphrase).

God has placed a mechanism in the Psalm 112 Man's house to generate substance, (a way of making money). This mechanism is that man's wealth because it has "generative power." You may not recognize it, but God has placed gifts and callings on the inside of you that will create wealth and riches in your house. That gift is the catalyst which creates the wealth in your house, and that wealth contains the generative power to create riches in your house.

Several years ago I was involved with an amazing church in Madison, Mississippi that I would describe as a "Missions Church." By that I mean that one of its primary reasons to exist was to support missionaries around the world in their calling to take the gospel to the people in their respective nations. These inspiring missionaries establish churches, operate Bible schools, take care of children in orphanages, respond to natural disasters, and a host of other things that missionaries do in proclaiming the gospel of Jesus around the world. This church consisted of a group of about 100 people who believed in the biblical principles of tithing and sowing and reaping. As a result, this church never had a financial problem. In addition to supporting missions, paying the church staff, and operating expenses, the church was able to acquire about 7 acres of land in a growing area of town with a small church located on it. The mortgage on the property was paid off in a relatively short period of time.

After operating for about ten years as a church with an emphasis on missions, the pastor and the board of directors of the church made the decision to discontinue operating as a typical church with services on Sundays and Wednesdays and to recommend that its members find other local churches to get involved with. There were a number of great churches in our area, and the consensus was that we should join ourselves to them, supporting their efforts to reach the lost.

I'm sure that other churches have closed their doors in the past with the members finding other churches to attend, but this was unusual. This church was not closing because of a church split or disagreements between its board or members. It was not closing because of a scandal of some sort, and it was not closing because of a lack of financial support. In fact, the church had no debt, and the piece of property the church owned was valued at $1 million.

The thing that made this church closing unique is that the church still operates today as a supporter of missions around the world just like it did when the church doors were open. The church provides the same financial support to missionaries that it did when they were a fully functioning church with members giving their tithes and offerings every week, except it no longer receives weekly tithes and offerings. How is it able to do this with no more financial support coming in? Psalm 112:3 is in operation! The church sold the property that it had been using over its ten years of operation, and the sale generated $940,000 in cash after selling expenses were deducted. This cash was then invested so that the church would generate regular investment income. The earnings from the investments are enough to continue supporting the missionaries at the same level that the church had been doing when it was in full operation. And what's more, the original principle balance has grown from $940,000 to over $1 Million.

I am telling this story to illustrate the difference between wealth (Hebrew - hon) and riches (Hebrew - ser). In this case, the $940,000 proceeds from the building sale was the wealth of the church. That wealth generates income (riches) that allows the church to continue to support missionaries around the world. Additionally, the invested amount (the wealth) continues to grow.

The sale of the property and the cash it produced was the mechanism that God gave the church to generate riches. If the church had spent all the building proceeds at the time of the sale, the wealth that was intended to generate riches would have disappeared, taking its power to generate riches with it.

Pastor John Osteen used to call this type of financial stewardship "Living off the Top of the Barrel." In other words, you don't spend your principle. You live off the income that the principle (or wealth) generates. In the case of the church that continues giving, even after it has closed its doors, they are living off the top. Their investments have generative power to produce. They are using the income generated by their investments to fund missions around the world. And this can go on indefinitely!

Since wealth has the generative power to produce riches, it can take many forms. It can be cash that is invested to produce more cash, or it can be a family business that produces income. It can be a talent or gift that produces income for the possessor like a musician or an actor. It can be a creative idea for a product that can be patented and sold or knowledge in a particular field that people are willing to pay to obtain. It could be property that is rented or land that contains timber that can be harvested. It can be something as simple as a snow cone machine that produces snow cones which are sold to generate income for the owner. God has promised that the Psalm 112 Man will have wealth, the generative power to produce riches, in some form. What is the wealth in your house?

IN THEIR HOUSES

"Wealth and riches shall be in their houses"(Psalm 112:3a). The Hebrew word translated "houses" is bayit and is not just a physical house. It is used to describe a family. If we used this word in the phrase, "The house of David is blessed", we would be saying that David and his descendants are blessed. So, if wealth and riches are in the house of the man that esteems God and His word, this tells us that family wealth can be passed down from one generation to another.

We sometimes see this with family businesses. A family business may be the wealth that contains generative power to produce income (riches), and when the children take over, the wealth continues to produce. Is it guaranteed that the wealth will not be squandered or spent by subsequent generations? Obviously not. Remember, it is the generation of the upright that is blessed (verse 2). The Psalm 112 Man, however, trains his children to honor and esteem the things of God, and as a result, wealth and riches can be passed from one generation to the next.

Sometimes wealth is passed to the next generation through the use of family foundations. There have been many very wealthy families that have established private foundations funded from the riches generated by the wealth in their houses and used to carry out the charitable wishes of the founders. Many of these foundations continue to be controlled by the lineal descendants of the founders.

In other cases, the Psalm 112 Man may just leave cash and other investments to his children that, if managed in a manner befitting a Psalm 112 house, will continue to produce more. We will look closer at this when we dive into verse 5 of this Psalm.

Proverbs 13:22 tells us, "A good man leaves an inheritance to his children's children." I like to say that a Psalm 112 Man leaves the wealth and riches in his house to be managed by his descendants. And, because his children have been trained in the Psalm 112 household, the benefits continue and bless many for generations. A Psalm 112 Man thinks generationally, not just in the present. Because of this, many generations are impacted.

THEIR RIGHTEOUSNESS ENDURES FOREVER

In the view of the Old Testament Hebrew people, a man's wealth was a sign of a man's right standing with God. If a man was right, just, and morally good in God's sight, it would be evidenced by the blessing on his house. The blessing on a man's house was essentially God's seal of approval of the man. As an example of this, take a look at the first chapter of the Book of Job. Verse 3 tells us that "He was the greatest man among all the people of the east." If you read verses 1-3 you will see that because of Job's honor and fear of God, he had amassed a considerable fortune. God confirms as much to Satan in verse 8 when he said, "Have you considered my servant Job? There is no one on earth like him; he is blameless and upright, a man who fears God and shuns evil."

The author of Psalm 112 gives us a deeper understanding of this concept. The wealth and riches in this man's house are a direct result of his heart towards God and His word. He is in right standing with God because he esteems and honors God and His word above all else. God's word is the foundational authority in his life. The Psalm 112 Man has faith in God and His promises just like Abraham did. Genesis 15:6 tells us, "Abraham believed the Lord, and he credited it to him as righteousness." Romans 4:3 in the New Testament quotes this scripture in establishing Abraham as the father of faith. In the New Covenant, we are made righteous and are justified by our faith in what Jesus accomplished for us. The New Living Translation says in Romans 3:22 that "We are made right with God by placing our faith in Jesus Christ." The Old Testament saints were given credit for being righteous by believing what God said (looking forward to the coming Messiah) and New Testament saints are made righteous by having faith in what the Messiah did. Righteousness (right standing with God) comes by faith in both cases. It comes by believing God.

The Psalm 112 Man is one that is righteous, not because of his own works, but simply because he believes what God has promised in His word and places his faith and trust in that word. How great is that? As believers, everything we have from God comes to us by faith. Our salvation comes by faith, our healing comes by faith, our peace and joy come by faith, and our financial well-being comes by faith. So how do we get faith for these things? Romans 10:17 tells us, "Faith comes by hearing, and hearing by the word of God." We get faith by hearing what God says about salvation, healing, joy, and peace, and financial well-being. As we continuously hear and meditate on the word (esteeming it highly), faith comes.

Since faith begins where the will of God is known, we have to know that it is God's will for wealth and riches to be in our houses. God's will is communicated to us by His word. And Psalm 112 tells us that wealth and riches will be in the house of those who esteem God and His word. Therefore we know it is God's will for wealth and riches to be in our houses if we make God and his word the foundational authority in our lives. By doing this we are also assured that our right standing with God will endure.

Some may be concerned that having wealth and riches will turn their hearts away from God. After all, I Timothy 6:10 says, "For the love of money is a root of all kinds of evil. Some people, eager for money, have wandered from the faith and pierced themselves with many griefs." Notice that it is the love of money that is the root of all evil. The Psalm 112 Man doesn't pursue money, he pursues God. The wealth and riches are a by-product of the Psalm 112 Man's pursuit of God. Matthew 6:33 is clear, "But seek first his kingdom and his righteousness, and all these things will be given to you as well."

Notice also that verse three tells us the righteousness of the Psalm 112 Man will endure forever. This comes immediately after the promise that wealth and riches will be in his house. For righteousness to endure, it had to be present already in the Psalm 112 Man's life. First came righteousness, then came wealth and riches. So we can conclude that wealth and riches came as a by-product of the Psalm 112 Man's right standing with God. He pursued God first, and wealth and riches followed.

When I realized that you could be wealthy and righteous at the same time, this changed everything for me. It was a true paradigm shift in my life. It is true, that one word from God can change your life forever. However, I have grown to discover there is much more to the Psalm 112 Man than just wealth, riches, and righteousness. The rest of Psalm 112 puts some meat on the bones of this man and provides a full picture of what the life of this wealthy and righteous man looks like.

CHAPTER 4

LIGHT DAWNS FOR THE UPRIGHT

Verse 4 – Even in darkness light dawns for the upright, for those who are gracious and compassionate and righteous.

You've probably heard the saying, "It's always darkest just before the dawn." You may have even used this saying to encourage friends or relatives facing difficult situations. By using this dawning of day analogy, you were letting them know that things would get better soon. However, while the sentiment is nice and may provide a degree of comfort to someone going through a difficult time, scientifically, it is not true. The darkest time of the night is actually when we are 180 degrees from the sun, halfway between sunset and sunrise. It is not darkest just before dawn. And while some believe that they are actually quoting scripture when they use these words, Thomas Fuller, the 17th century English theologian and historian, is actually the person given credit for this quote. I'm sure many have found consolation in these words, but the promise of God found in verse 4 of Psalm 112 provides far greater encouragement to those facing dark situations in their lives.

From a natural point of view, darkness is the absence of light. Trying to walk without enough light can cause us to stumble and fall and can cause damage to ourselves and others. Like me, you have probably tried to walk through your house at night with all the lights off, trying to remember where each piece of furniture is located. You inevitably end up stubbing your toe against a chair or bookcase. Walking in the dark usually does not end well. However, by shining a light on our path, darkness is removed and obstacles in our way are exposed and identified so we can continue on our way without harm.

Have you ever been in a situation where it seemed like you were in darkness? I'm not talking about physical darkness, but the absence of the light needed to determine which way to turn. It's the kind of darkness that creates stress and panic and a feeling of helplessness. It may seem like the situation is hopeless, and there was no way out. I'm talking about the kind of situation that paralyzes you in your tracks and keeps you up at night with thoughts of, "What am I going to do?" There seem to be no good options, only potentially bad outcomes. It's the kind of darkness that makes you feel like God is nowhere in sight and that he is oblivious to your cries for help.

I had a situation like that a couple of years after I received the encouraging word from the lady at our church, telling me I was a Psalm 112 Man. I had opened my CPA practice in 1988 after moving to Jackson, Mississippi with very little savings. In fact, we had cashed out our retirement plan when we moved to Jackson. We used the $32,000 from the plan as seed money to get our business off the ground because we knew it would take a while to get an income established. Things went well, and I began to take on a number of tax and accounting clients, providing a decent income for our family. It wasn't long before I added a staff member, then another, and then another. I should mention that from the first day, as had been my custom since I became a Christian at age 16, I tithed off of every dollar that I received. Robin and I agreed at the start of our marriage that we would be tithers. We even tithed off the gross income that our CPA firm received before deducting any salaries paid to staff or any other expenses. This was more than was actually required scripturally, but believed we were led by God to do this. In any event, the firm was prospering, and things were going well. Then came the "dark situation." We had a period of several months when some of my clients did not pay their bills on time. Although it was not true, it felt like my clients had gathered together and decided, as a group, not to pay me for a while. This created a very tight cash flow situation that came to a head with payday approaching for my staff. It looked like I was not going to be able to meet payroll, and my staff would not get paid. I made an all-out effort to collect from my past due clients, but to no avail. I did not have a bank credit line or other immediate source on which to draw funds to meet payroll. It seemed like the perfect storm. How would I ever be able to tell my staff that they were not going to get paid? Not only would this put them in a situation where they might not be able to pay their bills, but it might mean that they would have to go elsewhere to seek employment. They relied on me to pay them on payday. I could not blame them if they took another job. It could mean the end of my firm and my reputation as a business owner destroyed.

I went to my post office box twice daily during that week of payroll with the hope that a check would be in the mail, but to no avail. I told no one but my wife Robin about this very stressful situation, and the two of us had agreed together in prayer that somehow God would send us $10,000.00 in extra funds to get us through this period. We had no idea where the money would come from, but both of us knew the prayer of agreement between a husband and wife resulted in great power being made available to us. I remember sitting in my car at the post office parking lot thanking God that he would answer our prayer and somehow make a way. In retrospect, this was the most important thing I could do to see the light of God shine in my darkness. Still, at the time, it seemed there was no way out. It was a very dark week.

But then, on the day that payroll was due, light dawned in the middle of this darkness. I received a call from a friend (a brother in the Lord), telling me God had spoken to him and told him to give me $10,000.00. I could hardly believe my ears. $10,000! The exact amount that Robin and I had agreed on. I can't tell you how excited I was. Immediately Robin and I thought, "We should have asked for more!" However, this was more than enough to cover the payroll that week and to carry the firm over until the cash flow began to improve. God showed himself to us as a Way Maker that week. Light dawned for us in the middle of a dark hour and God's word in Psalm 112:4 became a reality in our lives.

Although there have been many other times that I have faced dark situations that required a breakthrough from God, I have not faced a situation quite like that one since, and I learned a few things about collecting receivables from clients that may have prevented this from happening in the first place. Even though my inexperience may have landed me in that dark situation, God was faithful to His word and provided a way out.

I John 1:5 tells us, "God is light; in him there is no darkness at all." And Psalm 119:105 says, "Your word is a lamp for my feet, a light on my path." There is always a way out for the Psalm 112 Man. Why? Because his whole life is anchored to the foundation of God's word and he trusts in the promises of God, including the promise contained in this verse. No matter how bleak and dark the situation may appear, for the upright man, light will arise in the middle of the darkness, and an answer will come. Never count the Psalm 112 Man out!

Even when there is darkness all around, light arises for the Psalm 112 Man. He does not have to wait until the world around him experiences the dawning of day. He receives light even when all others around are still groping in the dark. Remember Isaac who sowed in the midst of a famine? He reaped a one-hundred-fold return in the same year, even in the midst of darkness all around. Light arises for those who are in right standing with God.

Two words that describe the heart of a Psalm 112 Man are grace and compassion (or mercy). Because the Psalm 112 Man delights in the things of God, it should be no surprise that these two attributes are part of this man's makeup. Grace and compassion (mercy) describe the heart of God towards people, and as we meditate on God's word and spend time fellowshipping with Him, these two characteristics will emerge as well.

If there is one thing I have learned about our heavenly Father over the course of my life, it is that the gifts He gives to us are meant to benefit others as well as ourselves. The abilities, callings, and gifts that God has placed in our lives are there to bring others closer to Him. Don't get me wrong, I am not saying that we should not enjoy the blessings of God in our lives. We should! "God gives us richly all things to enjoy." (I Timothy 6:17 NKJV). Still, the gifts and callings of God in our lives are meant primarily for the benefit of others.

Because of this, grace and mercy will be in evidence strongly in the life of a Psalm 112 Man. The Hebrew word translated "grace" in Psalm 112 is hannan. To be gracious means to stoop or bend in kindness to an inferior and to show favor and mercy. The word translated "compassion" in this verse is raham and means to show mercy and love. We will look at some practical applications of this in the next chapter because this word is at the heart of a Psalm 112 Man's character. These two characteristics also epitomize God's heart toward man and the things that compelled him to send his son for us.

Those people who seek God and his kingdom first can expect for light to dawn in the darkness for them. This is the lifestyle of a Psalm 112 Man. There is nothing that can utterly overwhelm him. Nothing can keep him in darkness, and nothing can keep him from demonstrating the grace and mercy of God to those around him. Nothing can keep him from fulfilling God's plan for his life. His life is built upon the solid rock of God's promises, and because of that, God's light will always dispel the darkness that tries to envelope a Psalm 112 Man.

"Even in darkness, light dawns for the upright."

CHAPTER 5

WEALTH WITH A PURPOSE

Verse 5 – Good will come to those who are generous and lend freely, who conduct their affairs with justice.

When I read Psalm 112 for the first time, I stopped after I read verse 3 because it was such a revelation to me that you could be wealthy and righteous at the same time. However, once the seed of verse 3 had been securely planted in my heart and had taken root, I began to read and meditate on the other verses of Psalm 112. I found that there was much more to the Psalm 112 Man than just wealth, riches, and righteousness. There was, in fact, a purpose for that wealth.

I mentioned in chapter 4 that the Psalm 112 Man was full of grace and mercy that was directed towards others. As we drill down into verse 5, we discover the practical way in which the Psalm 112 Man allows the grace and mercy of God to flow through him.

Robin and I lived in Baton Rouge, Louisiana from 1981-1987. During the time we lived there, a television series was on the air entitled, "Lottery!". The show was on the air for only one season, but I watched every episode, fascinated with the storyline. The show revolved around two characters: one was a representative of the fictional Intersweep Lottery Company and the other an Internal Revenue Service agent. The two travelled around the country informing ticket holders that they'd won the lottery. The IRS agent went along to ensure that income taxes were paid on the winnings while the lottery representative gave the winner the exciting news. Most of the show dealt with how the winners handled the sudden wealth they had been given.

The thing that interested me the most about this television series was the guy that had the job of distributing the funds to the lottery winners and informing them that they had won. I remember thinking to myself, "I want to be that guy!" While many would long to be the person that was winning the lottery and receiving all that cash, my focus was on the one who was giving it away. This guy had a really amazing lifestyle. He travelled first class, dressed well, and ate well, but above all, he was making a huge impact in the lives of the people that won the lottery. He was a professional philanthropist. What a great job! I would much rather be the guy that could give all that money away than the guy that was receiving the money.

Acts 20:35 says, "It is more blessed to give than to receive." My brother-in-law and business partner, David White, has a different take on this verse. He says, "It is more blessed to be able to give than to have to receive." In other words, the one who already has and gives is already blessed more than the one who is receiving. That sentiment is how I felt about being the lottery distributor. I would rather be the one with the resources that can be given to help others than the one that needed to be helped.

DEALING GRACIOUSLY

Verse 5 describes the man that is doing just that with the wealth and riches that are in his house. The King James Version of this verse says, "A good man deals graciously and lends." As we saw in chapter 4, the word translated "graciously" means to stoop or bend in kindness to an inferior, showing favor and mercy. In the case of a Psalm 112 Man, he is willing to show favor and mercy to someone who does not have the resources that he has. His heart of compassion compels him to help where he can. The Apostle Paul describes this man in II Corinthians 9:8 when he says, "And God is able to bless you abundantly, so that in all things at all times, having all that you need, you will abound in every good work." This concept is totally contradictory to the idea that God has promised only to meet our needs. Don't get me wrong. God will meet all our needs, but He wants to go far beyond that! Not only will God meet our needs, he wants us to have more than enough to meet our needs and have an abundance left over to participate in every good work.

The Psalm 112 Man shows the favor and mercy of God through the distribution of his resources. He is not a hoarder; he is a distributor and a faithful steward of what God has placed in his hands. The Psalm 112 Man is a philanthropist!

Dealing graciously is more about our heart to help than anything else. In I Timothy 6:17-18, Paul tells Timothy, the young pastor at the church in Ephesus, to "Command those who are rich in this present world not to be arrogant nor to put their hope in wealth, which is so uncertain, but to put their hope in God, who richly provides us with everything for our enjoyment. Command them to do good, to be rich in good deeds, and to be generous and willing to share."

Notice that the rich, the Psalm 112 Man, should be willing to share. Someone who deals graciously is willing and has a heart to share. He wants to help others. He is not greedy or stingy, neither is he a hoarder trying to protect his stuff, but his heart is in his giving.

LENDING

In verse 5 we also see that the Psalm 112 Man lends freely. Initially, this verse created a problem for me. In my mind, lending was a bad thing, biblically speaking. Lenders seemed to be described as those who took advantage of people. Like many people, I thought the phrase, "Neither a borrower nor a lender be" was taken from scripture, but I found that it was not. It is actually a quote from William Shakespeare. It's amazing how we can go through life using sayings that we think are from the Bible in order to develop or support our theology and find later that those sayings were totally contrary to what the word actually says. But thank God for the light of His word that gets us back on track.

Lending in the Old Testament was encouraged among the Hebrews, but it was to be without interest. The Bible does warn us, however, that "the borrower is slave to the lender" (Proverbs 22:7) and that problems can arise when we act as a surety for someone else's debt. Additionally, the New Testament tells us to "Let no debt remain outstanding, except the continuing debt to love one another" (Romans 13:8). So, when Psalm 112:5 tells us that good will come to someone who lends freely and is gracious, is that in conflict with these other biblical warnings? What does it mean to lend in biblical terms?

The Hebrew word translated "lend" is lawa and means to twine as pieces of yarn are twisted together to form a strong piece of twine. It means to join oneself to someone else financially. Joining oneself to another financially does not necessarily mean lending in the traditional Western sense of the word. It means to take an interest in the financial need of someone else and to use our financial resources to help meet that need. To be joined to someone financially may mean making a contribution to a missionary for the construction of an orphanage or to support someone who is taking the gospel to an unreached part of the world. It may mean helping a family who is unable to work, or helping them cover some unexpected medical expenses, or it might even mean bending over on the city streets to give someone a couple of dollars to buy a meal. Whatever the purpose of the financial help, to "lend", in this context, is to join ourselves to someone financially to help them accomplish something that they cannot do without help.

By putting his money to work to benefit others, the wealth of the Psalm 112 Man gains purpose. The wealth in this man's house does more than just make his life comfortable. His wealth produces income which can be used to help others accomplish what God has called them to do. Now that is money with a purpose!

GOOD WILL COME

The NIV version of this verse says, "Good will come to those who are generous and lend freely, who conduct their affairs with justice." Good will come! What a powerful thought, that our generous giving causes good to be released to us. When I think of these words, I see waves of God's goodness being released and crashing over us. It's true that we are not saved by works or any good thing that we do. We are saved by grace through faith. However, good works certainly do have an impact on our lives. Being generous and lending freely will not purchase our eternal salvation, but generosity is a powerful spiritual force that has the ability to shake good things loose in our lives that have been delayed or restrained in their journey to reach us.

When we are led by God to be generous and give, many times the act of our giving will open doors that have previously been shut to us. This is God's goodness coming to us. We have seen it countless times in our lives. Our giving has opened the door to business opportunities that we would never have seen if we had not been obedient when prompted to give.

There is one particular missionary couple that we began partnering with nearly fifteen years ago to help them reach their African nation for Jesus. Since we began helping them fulfill their calling, the net worth of our company has increased by nearly 1000%! We believe good has come to us as a result of our giving and is what continues to propel our business forward. Good comes to us! We now have over twenty different missionaries and ministries that we partner with to help them accomplish what God has called them to do. These partnerships are key to seeing the goodness of God flowing in our businesses and in our personal lives.

Something powerful happens when we release this God-given spirit of generosity in our lives. Not only does good come as a result, there is also great joy in being able to help people fulfill God's plan and purpose for their lives.

Consequently, verse 5 is telling us, "Good will come to those who are willing to show favor, grace, and mercy to someone who lacks the needed resources by joining themselves to them financially, helping them accomplish something they are not able to do by themselves"(Psalms 112:5, author's paraphrase).

CONDUCTING OUR FINANCIAL DEALINGS WITH DISCERNMENT

The second part of this verse in the King James Version says that this man "guides his affairs with discretion"(Psalm 112:5b NKJV). By keeping this part of the verse in context with the first part of the verse, which refers to the Psalm 112 Man's involvement with other peoples' financial needs, we can conclude that the "affairs" that he is guiding or conducting with discretion are the dealings he has with others involving their financial needs. The discretion being exercised is not just in matters of helping others, but it is certainly the context in which it is used here.

The Hebrew word for "affairs" is dabar and is a very broad term that encompasses just about every aspect of our actions. The primary definition is "matters", and it includes what we say, how we respond, judgments we render, decisions we make, business transactions we enter into, counsel we give, etc. Essentially, dabar refers to the dealings and interactions we have with people as we go about our daily activities.

The Psalm 112 Man conducts and guides these activities with justice, discernment, and discretion. The writer of Psalm 112 does not want us to get the impression from the first part of this verse that the Psalm 112 Man is just throwing money around and giving indiscriminately. He exercises judgment, discernment, and discretion in his giving. He is able to discern what the good works are that the Apostle Paul describes in II Corinthians 9:8 when he says that we will "abound in every good work." This means that there are also works that would not be good for us to join ourselves to.

This is an extremely important aspect of the Psalm 112 Man. There is no shortage of need in this world, and we are all faced with decisions every day about whom we are going to join ourselves to financially. There are some good works that we need to be involved with and there are some not-so-good works that we need to stay away from. The Hebrew word that is translated "discretion" or "justice" is mispat and is best translated "verdict". As we are confronted with opportunities to get involved financially with someone in need, we are judging whether this is a good work for us or not and are pronouncing a verdict on each case as it comes to us. How do you distinguish a good work from a one that is not? How do you conduct your dealings in this area with discernment and the proper judgment? The following story may help to answer this question.

For 10 out of the last 18 summers, my wife and I have traveled to Chicago to attend a business conference. The conference generally lasts for three or four days and it has always been a great opportunity for the two of us to spend some time away from our normal environment and spend quality time with each other. During the day, while I am in class, my wife walks down Michigan Avenue and shops, and in the evenings, we go to dinner and then catch a show or just walk around and enjoy the beautiful summer weather along Lake Michigan. We both really look forward to the time together and enjoy the change from the slow pace that the big city hustle and bustle of Chicago brings.

There are downsides to the big city, however. Chicago's Michigan Avenue has an extraordinary number of people along the street asking for money from passersby. I suppose they have selected a good area, since this street is home to a large number of high-end retail shops and attracts many affluent people with money to spend. The people asking for money are mostly ignored by the people that see them every day as they walk to work, and they seem to be able to spot tourists and visitors a mile away. When they perceive that they have spotted a potential benefactor, some can get quite aggressive in their approach, engaging you in conversation as you walk by. Some will follow you until you either give in and cough up some cash or emphatically tell them to go away. Some of these people are real pros who operate this activity as a profitable business, and I would never suggest giving them money. However, there are some who are legitimately at rock bottom and need any help they can get. The problem is trying to discern the difference between the two.

This whole situation greatly bothered my wife, who has a mercy gift to begin with, and wants to help everybody. She would literally give everything she has in her purse to help those that ask her. She got to the point that she did not want to get out on the streets to shop during the day because she had to pass by the multitude of people that were asking for help, and her heart went out to them. She wanted to help them all, but how could she do that? She did not want to be taken advantage of, and she wanted to be led by God in her giving. When Robin gives a financial gift to someone who asks her, she wants to make a connection with them. She wants to look them in the eye and ask them if they know Jesus while she is giving them the money. Through the years, a number of people have prayed to receive Jesus as a result of her giving, and she had become pretty attuned to giving as God directed. But Michigan Avenue was just overwhelming to her. They were everywhere!

Finally, after several trips to Chicago and enduring the conflict about what to do with the people she encountered on the street, she decided that she would no longer struggle with who to give to. She would pray as she walked and listen to the Spirit of God and would believe Him for discernment and discretion as she passed the people on the street. She brought a large stack of $1, $5, and $10 bills that she would carry with her out of which she could give as she was prompted by the Holy Spirit. She was prepared and willing to give, and it became purposeful giving, not compulsive giving. It became great training in exercising discernment and discretion as she listened to the Spirit of God while walking down Michigan Avenue. As she passed by, she would "stoop down" (in most cases they were sitting down with a sign of some sort), and she would hand them a little money and tell them it was from Jesus and asked if they knew him. There was no pressure once she knew which person was a "good work" for her. It became a matter of whether she was being led by the Spirit or not. It's much easier to say "no", when you know the will of God. By praying and asking God for discernment, she no longer was under any compulsion to give. She was simply being a purposeful and cheerful giver as described in II Corinthians 9:7.

This is how the Psalm 112 Man and woman will "conduct their affairs with justice" (Psalm 112:5b). This example involved small amounts of money, but the principle is the same regardless of the size of the Psalm 112 Man's financial affairs. In order to render a proper verdict, we have to be led by the Spirit of God. Because the Psalm 112 Man loves God and his word and delights to do his will, he will make the right decisions about who and what to get involved with financially.

Considering the meaning of the Hebrew words used in verse 5, my translation is:

> "Good will come to the man who is willing to stoop down to help those who need what he has, using his resources to help them to accomplish what they cannot do on their own. He will exercise good judgment and discernment in determining how to deploy his resources" (Psalm 112:5, author's paraphrase).

CHAPTER 6

NEVER SHAKEN AND REMEMBERED

FOREVER

Verse 6 – Surely the righteous will never be shaken, they will be remembered forever.

We have read this word, "righteous" several times already in this short chapter, so it is obviously a key ingredient in what we observe about the life of this Psalm 112 Man. Every positive attribute that we observe about this man is tied to the description of him in verse 1. He delights in God and his word and everything that comes after that is because of this. He is righteous because he believes God and esteems every word that proceeds from his mouth. Verse six is no exception.

Those who hold onto and trust in the truth of God's word cannot be shaken. They cannot be moved away from God's purpose for them. Psalm 16:8 says, "I keep my eyes always on the Lord. With him at my right hand, I will not be shaken." Jesus' description of this is found in John 10:28, which says, "I give them eternal life, and they shall never perish; no one will snatch them out of my hand." The message is the same, those who follow after God cannot be moved off of the solid foundation they have established. Their life is founded on the solid rock. They will NEVER be moved or shaken.

The second part of this verse says that they will be remembered forever. How is this possible? FOREVER? There are some historical figures that are remembered for hundreds, and, in some cases, even thousands of years because we read about them in books, study them in school, or see memorials erected in their honor for some great thing they have done. When is the last time, however, that you thought about your great-grandfather? Do you know anything about him? Although there has been a resurgence in learning about our family histories through online searches and DNA testing, the memories and exploits of most of our forefathers have been lost. Don't get me wrong, they may have had a tremendous impact on our families and nations and the lives that we live today may not have been possible without them. However, even though they may have done incredible good during their lifetimes, they don't tend to live on in the memories of their descendants past a couple of generations unless they have done something famous.

No one wants to be forgotten. One of the worst feelings has to be the feeling that no one remembers the good you have done or even thinks about you. King David compared the trials he was facing with his enemies to one that has died and has been forgotten. "I am forgotten as a dead man, out of mind; I am like a broken vessel" (Psalm 31:12 NKJV).

So, what does God mean when he says the righteous who are not moved from their faith will never be forgotten?

Do you remember the story of Cornelius in chapter 10 of the Book of Acts? Cornelius was "a devout man and one who feared God with all his household, who gave alms generously to the people, and prayed to God always" (Acts 10:2 NKJV). God sent an angel to Cornelius to tell him to go to the Apostle Peter who would instruct him about what he should do. When the angel greeted Cornelius, he told him, "Your prayers and gifts to the poor have come up as a memorial offering before God" (Acts 10:4). God remembered his prayers and his offerings. God remembered the good deeds that he had done for the people in his name.

Although men may forget our giving, God will never forget. Our giving will live on forever, especially when our giving has made it possible for others to hear the gospel and respond. Eternity is a difficult concept for us to wrap our heads around, but the good we have done with our lives and our giving will be known and remembered in heaven for eternity. "…then, I shall know fully, even as I am fully known" (I Corinthians 13:12). Our righteous deeds will be known and remembered forever.

Another interesting fact about this verse is found in the Hebrew word translated as "never" and "forever." It is the same word. The word refers to eternity, or never ending. It describes eternity as the time period that the Psalm 112 Man will not be shaken and the time period that he won't be forgotten. What an amazing attribute about God. He will never forget our faith in him or the works that are done because of that faith.

As I understand scripture, the Judgement Seat of Christ is like an awards banquet in heaven. This is the place where Jesus will remember the good that we have done on the earth because of our faith in him. I can imagine Jesus saying, "I remember the time when you gave to this man's need or helped this lady accomplish this amazing thing." "God is not unjust; he will not forget your work and the love you have shown him as you have helped his people and continue to help them" (Hebrews 6:10). Jesus will never forget our work and labor of love and this will continue throughout eternity.

This is another promise to the man that fears the Lord and delights in his word.

> "He will never be moved, and he will never be forgotten" (Psalms 112:6, author's paraphrase).

CHAPTER 7

I DO NOT FEAR BAD NEWS!

Verse 7 – They will have no fear of bad news; their hearts are steadfast, trusting in the Lord.

My brother-in-law, David White, and I have been business partners for almost twenty years. Our offices are located side-by-side in our corporate headquarters and are connected by a pass-thru refreshment area. We use the pass-thru to go back and forth to each other's offices when we need to meet about something. Sometimes we get lazy and just yell back and forth rather than getting up and walking into the other person's office or calling on the telephone. There are doors that separate our offices from the pass-thru area, but they are seldom closed, which means we each can hear whatever is going on in the other's office most of the day.

David is as excited about Psalm 112 as I am, and we encourage each other often as we see this powerful psalm working in our families and in our businesses. Once, after receiving a phone call from someone who obviously delivered bad news to him, I heard David say out loud, "I do not fear bad news!" I had to laugh out loud even though I had no idea what news he had just received. Even now I do not remember what the news was about, but I knew he was just responding as a Psalm 112 Man would when faced with bad news. He knew whatever it was, God was able to turn it around to his benefit.

How we react to a bad report when we hear it is vitally important, and what we say at that moment can determine whether we end a trial in defeat or victory. A New Testament example of this is found in Mark 5. A man named Jairus had a daughter that was sick. He approached Jesus and asked him to come heal his sick daughter. As Jesus and Jairus were on their way to his house to tend to his daughter, they were delayed by the crowds and the healing of another woman. "While Jesus was still speaking, some people came from the house of Jairus, the synagogue leader. 'Your daughter is dead,' they said. 'Why bother the teacher anymore?' Overhearing what they said, Jesus told him, 'Don't be afraid; just believe.'"

Jairus had received a bad report about his daughter, and it does not get much worse than the news he had received. Jesus, hearing the bad report, immediately told Jairus not to fear, but to just believe. What was Jairus to believe? He was to believe that with Jesus, there is no situation too bleak for him to turn around. I can imagine the words that would have come out of Jairus's mouth if Jesus had not told him that. They would have been words of worry, doubt, and unbelief. The words would have been fear-based and not faith-based and could have kept Jairus from seeing victory in his situation.

The Bible does not record the words of Jairus at that point, but because they went on to Jairus's house and Jesus raised his daughter up, we have to conclude that Jairus responded to His words, rejected fear, and believed that Jesus could turn the situation around.

So how can a Psalm 112 Man be fearless in the face of bad news? The second part of this verse gives us the answer. "His heart is steadfast, trusting in the Lord" (Psalm 112:7b). The

Hebrew word translated steadfast is kun and can be translated "erect and prepared". This man's heart is prepared for any assault and stands erect when the bad news comes because he knows that God will take care of him. He trusts in the Lord. His foundation is built on the rock of the word of God. He knows the promises of God and that He will take care of him no matter what life or the enemy throws at him.

The key to developing a steadfast heart and trust in God is having the word of God in your heart. Joshua 1:9 tells us to meditate on the word day and night and then we will make our way prosperous and we will have good success. The Bible is full of promises that God has made to us that reveal his love and care for us. These promises are available to whomever dares to believe them. The Psalm 112 Man has made God and His word the foundation of his life. He delights in the promises that God has made to him and he trusts God. That is why his heart stands erect and prepared for any news that may come that is contrary to the promises of God. He knows God will deliver him!

"He does not fear bad news because his heart is steadfast, trusting in the Lord" (Psalm 112:7, author's paraphrase).

CHAPTER 8

THIS ENDS IN VICTORY!

Verse 8 – Their hearts are secure, they will have no fear, in the end they will look in triumph on their foes.

Have you ever used the phrase, "My heart is not in it"? I have. My brother-in-law and I are both instrument-rated private pilots, and we used to fly a Piper Saratoga, single engine airplane. We are also licensed as helicopter pilots. Obtaining our helicopter licenses was a long process that required much commitment and time in the helicopter away from our families and business. When the day came that we passed our flight exam and officially became helicopter pilots, it was a day of extreme satisfaction for having accomplished a goal that had been in our hearts for a couple of years. However, staying safe and current in a helicopter (or any aircraft) requires many hours of consistent flight time and more time away from the other things you enjoy doing. It became difficult to squeeze enough time into our schedules to stay current in both the helicopter and airplane. One day, while driving to lunch and discussing this, I said, "You know, my heart is really not in this any longer." David agreed and said he felt the same way.

Within a few hours we had made the decision to stop flying and sell both the airplane and the helicopter.

Our hearts were no longer in it. When someone uses that phrase, it means that their mind, will, and emotions are not supporting what they are doing. Our hearts being "in" something, fully engaged and committed, is essential to the success of whatever we do. And when our hearts are not in it, the outcome of any endeavor is usually not positive or beneficial. In order for us to be truly successful at most things in life, our hearts need to be fully engaged and supportive.

The term heart in verse 8 and in this popular phrase have the same meaning. It means the center or core of our being. The heart contains our will, emotions, and intellect, and is what drives our actions and ensures our success. It is our core that Paul was referring to when he told the Corinthians not to be conformed to this world, but to be transformed by the renewing of their minds. He was saying not to let the world be the thing that controls and influences your heart. Let your heart be shaped, molded, and strengthened by the word of God.

When verse 8 tells us that the heart of the Psalm 112 Man is secure, it is saying the core of his being is secure. The King James Version uses the term established rather than secure, but the Hebrew word is the same, samak, and means to be propped up by or leaning on something for stability and security so as not to be moved. The Psalm 112 Man's core being is leaning on and being propped up by the words that God has spoken to him. Those words keep him from being moved away from, losing interest in, or giving up on God's best for his life. A person with a secure heart will keep his eyes on the prize.

In verse 7, the heart of the Psalm 112 Man is described as, steadfast, which we noted meant to stand erect and prepared. In verse 8, his heart is described as secure or established, which means propped up and leaning upon something for stability and security. The two descriptions are complimentary and have the same result, no fear.

Because the Psalm 112 Man trusts in God and his word, the core of his being stands erect and is prepared and cannot be moved. He is leaning on and trusting in the word of God. He will not be moved or shaken from seeing the purposes of God fulfilled in his life. Because his trust is in God, fear has no place in his life. He stands fearless in the face of bad reports or attacks from the enemy of his soul, knowing that the end of the matter will be victory! In the end he will look in triumph on his foes. No matter what report comes his way, he does not fear because he knows that it will end well for him. God is his refuge and fortress.

My wife Robin and I had an opportunity to test this scripture in our lives in 2016. I was diagnosed with prostate cancer in October of that year. The doctors originally suspected just an infection, but after taking medication for this assumed infection for six weeks, my PSA numbers only got worse. It was determined that a biopsy of my prostate was in order. Robin and I had every confidence that the biopsy would show no cancer when we were called to the doctor's office to discuss the results. This, however, was not the case. He told us that I had prostate cancer, and that it was a very aggressive form that rated high on the Gleason Scale. The medical protocol for this was to have my prostate removed right away before the cancer could spread to other parts of my body. It was a complete surprise to us. We were fully expecting him to tell us there was no sign of cancer.

I have to tell you, there was no fear upon receiving that bad report, only surprise and disappointment that we did not hear the news we were expecting. We did not say much until the doctor left the room. We just tried to process the bad report that we had just been given. However, as soon as the doctor left the room and Robin and I were alone together, we looked at each other and simply said, "By the stripes of Jesus we are healed." Even though the bad report had not changed we knew that this would end in victory for us. Robin told me some time after this event that God had dropped a spirit of faith into her heart, and she did not fear. We never doubted that I was going to be healed, and when fear tried to raise its ugly head, we just spoke the word and refused to fear, trusting in Him. This is precisely what verse 8 is describing about the Psalm 112 Man. We had been putting the word of God in our hearts for years, and it was propping up our heart. The word was keeping our core erect and supported, so that when we were assaulted with a bad report, we had no fear, and we were not moved away from God's promise to us.

As a side note, in the weeks prior to this bad report, our pastor had been preaching a series of messages on the "Golden Texts of God's Word." These were scriptures that every believer should have in their arsenal (their hearts) as they live their lives in this world. The scripture that he used just before the bad report was delivered was I Peter 2:25 that tells us, "By his wounds you have been healed." This scripture had been propping up our core and keeping our heart secure when the bad report came. Where you go to church and the word that you are putting in your heart is extremely important. It can mean the difference between life or death and between faith and fear when you are faced with bad news.

Without getting into all the details of the two months that followed, I sought alternative medical treatment that involved immunotherapy, and today there is no evidence of cancer in my body. I still have my prostate, and we are looking in triumph upon our enemy. Had we reacted in fear when the bad report came, and had we not had secure hearts propped up by the word of God, I am not sure we would have had the same outcome. Thank God for his word and for Psalm 112!

> *Their hearts are secure, they will have no fear, in the end they will look in triumph on their foes. (Psalms 112:8, author's paraphrase)*

CHAPTER 9

DISTRIBUTING FREELY

Verse 9 – He has distributed freely; he has given to the poor; his righteousness endures forever; his horn is exalted in honor.

"Give until it hurts!" Have you ever heard this phrase used when money is being raised? Although fundraisers use this phrase to encourage people to give more money, the quote originates with Mother Teresa, who used it to describe the giving of love to others, not the giving of money in a fundraiser. You have probably been in a situation where you felt you were being pressured or manipulated into giving. It has happened to most of us at some time in our lives. I have given under pressure before, and it is not a good feeling. There is no joy in it, and it leaves you feeling like you have been robbed or have thrown your money away. However, as I grow in living as a Psalm 112 Man, I am discovering how to "distribute freely" as a Psalm 112 Man does.

When a Psalm 112 Man gives, he does so with joy and excitement. The Apostle Paul advocated this kind of giving in

57

one of his letters to the Corinthians in the New Testament. Paul was a Psalm 112 Man if there ever was one, and even quotes Psalm 112:9 in his writings. II Corinthians 9 serves as a companion chapter to Psalm 112 that confirms and amplifies what Psalm 112 living is all about. "Let each one give [thoughtfully and with purpose] just as he has decided in his heart, not grudgingly or under compulsion, for God loves a cheerful giver [and delights in the one whose heart is in his gift] (2 Corinthians 9:7 AMP). This is exactly the kind of giving (distributing freely) that Psalm 112:9 describes and is what is meant when Paul told Timothy to instruct the wealthy people in his church to be "ready to give and willing to share" (1 Timothy 6:18b NKJV).

To distribute freely means to give without pressure or a feeling of reluctancy. My advice to anyone who is feeling pressured to give is this, "Don't do it!." A gift given under pressure is not the kind of giving that makes God happy, nor is it one that will bring the harvest of righteousness that accompanies God-directed giving. God is looking for cheerful givers whose hearts are in their giving, and who delight in seeing the needs of others met. The Greek word for cheerful in this verse is hilaros from which we get the word hilarious. Distributing freely the Psalm 112 way is fun! When we give cheerfully, we are allowing the love of God, the original giver, to flow through us. "For God so loved the world that he gave…" (John 3:16).

A WORD ABOUT THE TITHE

I should probably point out that giving or distributing in this verse is not the same thing as tithing. The giving described in Psalm 112 and in II Corinthians 9 is not the giving of God's tenth to the local church. The giving described in these verses is after the tithe. The first ten percent belongs to God. We should never get bogged down in legalism with our money, but there are still certain truths and principles to be followed when it comes to managing our money. You cannot become a Psalm

112 giver if you are not returning to God what belongs to him in the first place. By bringing the tithe into the storehouse, we acknowledge that God is the one who provides and takes care of us. It is the foundation of any successful Psalm 112 household, and without it, the walls of our wealth-filled financial house will never be built.

This book is not intended to be about the tithe, and I will leave it to you, the reader, to settle the matter in your own heart whether the tithe is a principle that is applicable to New Testament believers. However, I will provide a couple of scriptural principles that form the basis for my belief that the tithe is for believers today.

The tithe is such an important aspect of our financial well-being that God tells us in Malachi 3:10 to "Test him in this." Nowhere else in scripture does God tell us to prove him or put him to the test. The Nation of Israel was facing financial ruin because they were not honoring God in the tithe. God told them they had been robbing him by withholding the tithe. If they would only begin to tithe again, they would see the windows of heaven opened and overwhelming blessings poured out on their nation. God would rebuke the devourer that had been destroying their crops, and they would once again become a fruitful and blessed land. In fact, all the nations around them would see what God would do for them and call them blessed.

Some say that this is an Old Covenant principle and no longer applies because, as Christians, we are no longer under the Law of Moses and are not expected to keep all the provisions of that law. However, the principle of tithing originated before the Law of Moses. Abraham gave tithes to Melchizedek in Genesis 14:19, and Jacob promised to give God a tenth of all that God gave him if he would provide for him and bring him back to the land of his fathers (Bethel) in Genesis 28:20-22. Solomon also tells us in Proverbs 3:9 to honor the Lord with our substance and with the first fruits of all of our increase. Solomon was not quoting the Law of Moses; he was giving us a practical guide for living a blessed life.

The principle of tithing is also endorsed by Jesus himself in Mathew 23:23 when he told the Pharisees that they were right to tithe, but they were ignoring other important matters of the Law. In Hebrews 7, the writer discusses the fact that Abraham gave tithes to Melchizedek, a type and model of Jesus. In Hebrews 7:8, we are told that it is Jesus who receives the tithe now and by tithing we proclaim that Jesus lives. "In the one case, the tenth is collected by men who die; but in the other case, by him who is declared to be living." By tithing, we are declaring that Jesus lives and that he is well able to provide for us.

Some might say, "If I tithe first, there will not be any left over to give", but that is where trusting the word comes in. If we don't act on what the word declares about the tithe, we prevent the abundance of God from flowing in our lives. Wealth and riches are blessings of God that come from delighting in God's word and honoring his word and precepts, including the God-given principle of the tithe. Honoring God with our first fruits prepares the way for our barns to be filled with plenty, and then, we can step over into real giving! The wealth in our house produces an abundance and allows us to give generously out of the abundant overflow that God brings into our lives. After all, II Corinthians 9:8 tells us, "God is able to bless you abundantly, so that in all things at all times, having all that you need, you will abound in every good work." The tithe is where this abundance begins.

GIVING TO THE POOR

What does it mean to give to the poor? The Hebrew word translated poor in this verse is ebyon and means someone who is in need or experiencing lack. I mentioned earlier that the Apostle Paul quoted Psalm 112:9 in II Corinthians 9:9. The context in which Paul quotes this verse involves an offering the Corinthian church had promised to give to the believers in Jerusalem who were suffering great persecution and lack. They were in need, and the Corinthian church wanted to give. Paul was sending Titus to collect the offering they had promised a year earlier, and this letter was urging them to be ready to give when Titus arrived.

It is in this context that we learn what it means to be a Psalm 112 giver, and it reveals the purpose of a Psalm 112 Man's wealth. II Corinthians 9:6-15 is presented below to allow us to get the picture of what a Psalm 112 Man's giving looks like.

"Remember this: Whoever sows sparingly will also reap sparingly, and whoever sows generously will also reap generously. Each of you should give what you have decided in your heart to give, not reluctantly or under compulsion, for God loves a cheerful giver. And God is able to bless you abundantly, so that in all things at all times, having all that you need, you will abound in every good work. As it is written: (this is written in Psalm 112:9, author's note)

"They have freely scattered their gifts to the poor;
    their righteousness endures forever."

Now he who supplies seed to the sower and bread for food will also supply and increase your store of seed and will enlarge the harvest of your righteousness. You will be enriched in every way so that you can be generous on every occasion, and through us your generosity will result in thanksgiving to God. This service that you perform is not only supplying the needs of the Lord's people but is also overflowing in many expressions of thanks to God. Because of the service by which you have proved yourselves, others will praise God for the obedience that accompanies your confession of the gospel of Christ, and for your generosity in sharing with them and with everyone else. And in their prayers for you their hearts will go out to you, because of the surpassing grace God has given you. Thanks be to God for his indescribable gift!"

The situation that existed in the Jerusalem church was not a permanent condition of the believers in Jerusalem, but at that time, they were in need. They were needy, and God used the resources of the Corinthian believers to meet the needs of the believers in Jerusalem. They had an abundance not only to meet their own needs but to help meet the needs of others. That is money with a purpose!

There are needs around us every day that far surpass our abilities to help. So how do we decide whom to help? This is not always an easy thing to decide. Paul told the Corinthians that God would enrich them so they could be generous on every occasion! The King James Version says you will have an abundance for every good work. The work that I am called to do may be different than the work you are called to do, and a good work for you may be different than a good work for me. A good work for you is the one that God has called you to, and it may not be the same work that God has called me to.

There are certain opportunities that God may draw me to that are of no interest to you and vice-versa. If you want to make sure you are giving to the good work that God has ordained for you, my advice is to listen for his voice. Jesus said, "My sheep listen to my voice; I know them, and they follow me" (John 10:27). Verse 5 of that chapter tells us that they will not follow a stranger because they do not know his voice.

It can be difficult to say "no" to someone who is asking for help, especially when the need is great or genuine. There are many needs and many opportunities that look like good works, but they might not be ones that God is directing you to. Remember, the Psalm 112 Man does not give under compulsion, but as he has purposed in his heart. He gives freely and with an anointing to do so by God. It is easier to say, "no", when you know in your heart that it is not something God wants you to do. Stay willing to distribute, but listen to his voice and be led by the peace of God.

We recently gave a significant amount of money to a project to win the lost to Jesus. To make a long story short, it was not very successful. We knew and respected the people that were organizing and fundraising for the event and agreed to help in the project because of that respect. We were not involved in the planning or implementation of the project and were unaware that certain elements of the plan had changed after we had made our financial commitment. These changes were devastating to the plan's success, and when the day arrived for the event, the actual crowds for the event were a fraction of what had been projected early in the planning stages. There were a few people that received Jesus as a result of the event, which is a wonderful thing, but when the expectations were for hundreds or even thousands to receive Christ, the actual results were disappointing.

Had we known then what we know now, we would never have given toward the event. This was not a good work for us. I would have to say in retrospect that we allowed ourselves to give out of compulsion and out of respect for the people who were doing the event. We were not giving because we were directed by God to do so. Lesson learned. Always be led by God in your giving and not by the need. Sometimes, "NO", is the right response.

HIS RIGHTEOUSNESS ENDURES FOREVER

The second part of this verse "His righteousness endures forever", connects verse 9 with verse 3. Both verses contain this exact phrase. Verse 3 describes the wealth and riches that are in the house of the Psalm 112 Man and verse 9 describes what the Psalm 112 Man does with those riches. It connects wealth and purpose. In both verses, the righteousness of the man is described as enduring forever.

It was a mind-blowing revelation to me when I read in verse 3 that a man could be wealthy and righteous at the same time, but I now see why that is true. It is obvious from looking at verse 9 that the wealth and riches this man possesses do not possess him. It is true that God does not have any problem with us having stuff, as long as the stuff does not have us. If a man is able to distribute his earthly goods freely, his goods do not have a hold on him. If he is able to give joyfully to others as God directs, then that man's heart toward money is right. If he is ready to give and willing to distribute as I Timothy 6:18 admonishes, then the wealth and riches possessed by that man does not prevent that man from having a heart that is fully devoted to God.

If you remember the story of the rich young ruler who came before Jesus in Matthew 19:16-22, you will remember the young man told Jesus that he had kept all the commandments since his youth, but he wanted to know what else he needed to do to have eternal life. Jesus told him that he lacked one thing. What was the one thing that he lacked? Rather than telling the wealthy young man what he lacked, Jesus gave him something to do that would prove what was lacking. He told him to sell all that he had and give to the poor, and he would have treasure in heaven, and then to come and follow him. He asked him to do the one thing that he knew was keeping the young man from committing himself fully to God, his riches. His riches had him rather than him having the riches. Verse 22 tells us that he went away sad because he had great wealth. We might even infer from the young man's response that he went away sad because the great wealth had him.

Jesus was not saying that everyone has to sell all they have and give to the poor in order to have eternal life. However, for this young man, his wealth was a stumbling block that was keeping him from following Jesus with his whole heart. Following Jesus is about surrendering our lives to him, including those things that would keep us from fully serving him. After the rich man went away sorrowful, Jesus made the statement to his disciples in verse 23, "Truly I tell you, it is hard for someone who is rich to enter the kingdom of heaven." I'm sure that statement is true.

I met Jesus when I was sixteen years old and did not have a penny to my name. I lived at home with my parents and had all my needs met. But on my own I had nothing, except maybe a small savings account, where I put what was left of my meager paycheck from my summer job after I paid tax and my entertainment expenses. I was certainly not wealthy. My family and I were members of a United Methodist Church in Huntington, West Virginia and I had been hearing the message of salvation my whole life. When that message finally reached my heart through the girl I was dating (now my wife), there were no riches pulling on my heart to keep me from following Jesus. I don't know what it would have been like if I had been a rich young ruler with great wealth or even a 50-year-old man that had accumulated some wealth when I finally realized I needed a savior. I am eternally grateful to God that I heard the message when I was young and without possessions and that I did not have anything to keep me from saying yes to Jesus. The wealth and riches that have come to my house have all happened after the heart issue about money had been settled in my life.

It is a shame that some people miss out on what God has for them simply because they have misapplied a scripture like the one about the rich young ruler. God has no problem with you having wealth as long as that wealth does not occupy the place in your heart reserved for him.

The wealth in the house of the Psalm 112 Man is in its proper place, not in the place reserved for God. That is why the

Psalmist can say, "Wealth and riches are in their houses, and their righteousness endures forever" (Psalm 112:3). He proves this point by also saying, "They have freely scattered his gifts to the poor, their righteousness endures forever" (Psalm 112:9).

HONORING THE SOURCE OF OUR WEALTH

This last line of Psalm 112:9 is very interesting. "Their horn is lifted high in honor." How can the Psalm 112 Man's horn be lifted high? Men don't have horns, and not all play musical instruments, so obviously there is some other meaning. The Hebrew word translated "horn" is qeren, and can be translated as an animal horn, a musical horn, the projections from an altar, or figuratively, referring to someone's strength. In this case, the Psalmist is referring to the strength of the Psalm 112 Man.

What is the strength of the Psalm 112 Man? His strength is in God and his word. It is his trust and reliance on God's word that makes the Psalm 112 Man strong. Psalm 20:7 says, "Some trust in chariots and some in horses, but we will trust in the name of the Lord our God."

You will never hear the Psalm 112 Man boast about his greatness or his skills. You will never hear him say, "My power and the might of my hand have gained me this wealth" (Deuteronomy 8:17 NKJV), because, "By humility and the fear of the LORD are riches, and honor, and life" (Proverbs 22:4 NKJV).

The strength of the Psalm 112 Man's life is the Lord, and he knows it. He knows that without him, he is nothing. He is also not ashamed to lift high the one who gave him the wealth in his house and to give credit and honor to whom it is due.

The Psalm 112 Man is not impressed with himself because he knows from whom his wealth and success in life come. To believe that he has done it himself under his own might and power would make him a fool.

Thomas Tusser is given credit for saying, "A fool and his money are soon parted." Someone has added an extension to this saying, "I'm not sure how the two ever got together in the first place." Psalms 14:1 says, "The fool says in his heart, 'There is no God.'" I might add that a fool says in his heart, "God is not the source of my wealth." Thomas Tusser was right. To deny the source of our wealth and not honor the one to whom honor is due, makes one a fool.

"He has freely distributed his goods to the those in need and, thus, has shown that his heart is in lockstep with God's, understanding the purpose of his wealth; He also gives honor to God as the source of his wealth" (Psalm 112:9, author's paraphrase).

CHAPTER 10

THE PLANS OF THE WICKED

Verse 10 – The wicked will see and be vexed; they will gnash their teeth and waste away; the longings of the wicked will come to nothing.

We have an enemy! However, he is not our boss, our co-worker, our neighbor, a family member, or any other human being that we can see or touch. Our enemy is Satan, the devil, or, as he is sometimes called, the wicked one. He is the one who attempted to destroy Jesus at every turn during his earthly ministry, and he is the one who wants to stop you from fulfilling God's plan and purpose in your life. Our enemy does not want to see the seed of the word of God take root in our hearts. That seed has the power to transform our lives and impact the nations for good. The thought of us becoming Psalm 112 Men and Women terrifies him, and he will introduce stumbling blocks along our path or shoot fiery darts our way to try to prevent that from happening.

We should not be ignorant of Satan's devices to try to steal the word of God out of our hearts, and we should recognize the source of the attempts to remove us from the good path that we are traveling. Many times we blame people, bad luck, or even God when things happen in our lives that seem to take us off our path. We need to remember that the devil is the one that comes to steal, kill and destroy, and that he is our enemy, not God or other people. The devil is a thief, but God is a way maker! What the devil intends for harm, God will turn to our good. Our pastor, Joel Sims, preached a message recently in which he proclaimed, "If it is not good, it's not God!" That is a great litmus test to use in determining when to stand our ground against the attacks of the enemy.

Back in 2010, the Affordable Care Act was enacted and signed into law. This new law totally changed how the insurance industry operated and literally put some insurance companies and insurance agencies out of business. The law had the effect of eliminating commissions paid to insurance agents that sold major medical insurance plans and also eliminated the ability of companies to offer certain insurance policies that did not meet the restrictive guidelines under the new law.

We own an agency that generated commissions from the sale of major medical products, and we own an insurance company that sold products that it appeared could no longer be sold. In fact, the insurance product that would have been eliminated under the new law was our flagship product that generated significant income for the company. It looked like this new law could be our downfall and the end of a very successful business operation that was making a tremendous impact in our community and around the world through our giving.

Thankfully David and I, along with our wives and family, knew that the devil was a thief and God was a way maker. We recognized that what the devil meant for harm, God was able to turn to our good. People would ask us, "What are you going to do?" We even had thoughts of our own, "Could this be the end?" We never allowed the devil to get a foothold, however, by saying anything contrary to what the promises of God declared. We would say, "We don't care what changes in the law take place, we are still going to be profitable and come out on top. This new law will not prevent us from being successful. In fact, we will sell more than we ever have."

I am sure our words in response to his attack caused our enemy to gnash his teeth, and I also believe our words were the key to our victory in this attack. God gave the management and key employees witty ideas about how to re-make our agency that more than offset any lost commissions that occurred because of the Affordable Care Act. That agency today is more profitable than it has ever been. He also gave us ways that we could make our flagship product acceptable under the new law, and we are selling more than ever. In the process, God gave us ways to make money on other products that were not subject to the new law. The net worth of the company has increased to seven times what it was when the new law was enacted, and our giving and impact have both increased significantly. Only God can take what the devil, our enemy, meant for harm and turn it into a great victory!

Not everyone is going to be excited that you have discovered the truths contained in this psalm and begin to declare that wealth and riches are in your house. Some may even say to you, "You are only after money." or "You are just trying to get rich." Don't allow these words to steal the word out of your heart. Remember, your real enemy (the devil) is the one trying to keep you from becoming all that God has called you to be, and he is behind the opposition we face in getting there.

Jesus tells us in Mark chapter 4 that as soon as the word is planted in our hearts, the enemy comes immediately to try to steal that word away before it can take root. He knows that if the seed of the word (in this case, Psalm 112) takes root in our hearts, we will do great damage to his kingdom.

John 10:10 tells us, "The thief comes only to steal and kill and destroy; I am come that they may have life and have it to the full." We find in the Book of Acts, "How God anointed Jesus of Nazareth with the Holy Spirit and with power, who went about doing good and healing all who were oppressed by the devil, for God was with him." (Acts 10:38 NKJV) The Greek word translated "doing good" is euergeteo and means to be philanthropic and bestow benefits. Being philanthropic involves the giving of money, and the definition of a philanthropist is a person who seeks to promote the welfare of others, especially by the donation of money to good causes. When Jesus was "doing good", he was being philanthropic. He helped people financially!

Jesus's ministry obviously had funds to disburse because he had a treasurer, Judas, who managed the money. You don't have a treasurer to watch over the money unless you have money. Judas got upset when Mary broke the alabaster box of oil to anoint the feet of Jesus, saying that the money could have been used to give to the poor. When Judas left the last supper abruptly, some of the disciples assumed that he had gone to give money to the poor. So apparently, this was something that Jesus routinely did as part of his ministry.

Jesus made a mess of Satan's kingdom during his ministry on earth by doing good and healing people whose lives the devil had tried to destroy. He totally disarmed the forces of darkness in his death, burial, and resurrection.

When we allow the word to grow in our hearts and become all that God has called us to be, we continue the ministry of Jesus on the earth, doing good and healing those whom Satan has tried to steal from, kill, and destroy. After all, Jesus said, "Very truly I tell you, whoever believes in me will do the works I have been doing, and they will do even greater things than these, because I am going to the Father." (John 14:12)

As we become Psalm 112 Men and Women, and our families begin doing good in the Acts 10:38 sense of the word, it causes Satan great anguish and grief (Verse 10 – "The wicked will see it and be grieved,") and there will be times that his anguish and grief are expressed through people. We see this in the life of Jesus as he went about doing good. He was criticized by the religious leaders for doing good and for speaking the truth. Early in his ministry, these leaders were plotting together to find a way to destroy Jesus. The people that opposed Jesus and wanted to stop him were being influenced, and in many cases, controlled by Satan.

OPPOSITION TO THE WEALTHY

We should not be surprised when we face opposition from people when we begin to operate as Psalm 112 Men and Women. John 15:20 says, "Remember what I told you: 'A servant is not greater than his master.' If they persecuted me, they will persecute you also."

Have you noticed that a large part of the US population has a great dislike for wealthy people? You don't have to look far to find an example of this. Although President Donald Trump may be disliked by many for any number of reasons, he is disliked by a large number of Americans just because he is wealthy. During his 2016 Presidential campaign, you could hear Donald Trump say on many occasions, "I am very rich!" I got the feeling that he was saying this to get a rise out of his opponents that did not like the fact that he was wealthy. It worked! Entire political campaigns are built around the promise of the candidate to provide more "free stuff" to voters by taking money from the rich. The rich are portrayed as evil people who need to be punished. Some rich people may, in fact, be evil and may use their wealth in ways that harm rather than help those who are in need, but a large portion of the wealthy in this country use their wealth for good and for philanthropic purposes. It is certainly the case in the life of a Psalm 112 person.

Even the wealthy who are very philanthropic are criticized. Regardless of how much they give away or how many people they help, there are always those who think they should do more or help someone other than the ones they are helping. (It's easy to spend someone else's money!)

The Psalm 112 Man uses discretion and good judgment in his giving, which involves saying "no" sometimes to those who have a need, even in the face of criticism and opposition. The Psalm 112 Man is led by God in his giving and uses good judgment in choosing his good works. Sometimes criticism will come as a result of his choices. It comes with the territory, however, and the Psalm 112 Man needs to remain confident in his decisions and in what he believes and press on in the midst of the criticism and opposition.

One could logically ask, why would anyone criticize or persecute someone for doing good? I'm sure that same thought came to the minds of the disciples as they witnessed the good that Jesus did, and yet, while doing good, received the anger and criticism of the religious leaders. The answer is that the persecution and criticism are actually coming from our enemy, Satan. He just has to work through people to express his criticism and anger.

The Psalm 112 Man or woman has to settle it in their hearts early that our fight is not against people, it is against the spirit behind the people. Regardless of the criticism or persecution that comes as a result of having wealth in your house, we have to focus on our purpose and not be sidetracked by the strategies of the enemy.

OUR ENEMY WILL MELT AWAY

Verse 10 goes on to say that even though our enemy may be angry and express that anger towards us to try to get us off track, his rantings will come to nothing. "They will gnash their teeth and waste away." The New King James version of this verse uses the word "melts away." When I read this part of the verse about the wicked "melting away", I get the picture of the Wicked Witch of the East melting away at the end of the

"Wizard of OZ" movie, exclaiming, "I'm melting!"

This is a picture of the end of our enemy. Regardless of how much he hates us and wants to prevent us from doing the works of God, his plans will come to naught. They will melt away!

Be strong and courageous because…

> *"The longings of the evil one will come to nothing."*
> *(Psalm 112:10, author's paraphrase)*

A FEW MORE THINGS

As I came to the end of chapter 10, I realized there were some points about living the Psalm 112 life that I either had been unable to weave into any of the book so far or had under-emphasized their importance. So I thought I would include an epilogue of sorts to make sure these points were covered.

DREAM BIG

Many believers never experience the great life that God has available for them simply because they fail to dream. God wants to give us the desires of our hearts, and he wants us to see our dreams come true. After all, if you are a believer and love God, He is the one that placed those desires and dreams on the inside of you in the first place. Don't let those dreams slip simply because you don't see how it can happen.

Remember, our God is a way maker and has great experience in taking things that seem impossible and making them a reality. If all your dreams and desires have come true, it's time to pick up some new ones.

There is someone waiting for your dreams to come true because you are an answer to their prayers. There is a missionary somewhere that needs you to be the Psalm 112 Man and the philanthropist that God is calling you to be.

IT MAY NOT HAPPEN OVERNIGHT

Your dreams may not come true overnight. My dreams of being a Psalm 112 Man are still in the process of fulfillment. You will find that as you meditate on the promises of God and make them a part of your daily meditation and declaration, your dreams will get bigger. They will expand. As you begin to see a manifestation of what you have been dreaming about, what once looked impossible looks small, and you will set your sights higher.

To get there, however, you will need to feed continuously on the promises of God. Like Joshua, you will need to meditate on them day and night. As you do that, your faith and expectation will grow until one day, you will look yourself in the mirror and see the Psalm 112 Man you have become.

DOING THE WORKS OF JESUS

When you begin to operate as a Psalm 112 Man or woman, you are actually doing what Jesus did. Acts 10:38 tells us that Jesus went about "doing good." This meant Jesus went about being a philanthropist, one that used his money to bestow benefits on others. Jesus was anointed by God to do this. We can also do good under the anointing of the Holy Spirit.

This is impossible to do if you are not making ends meet yourself. God never intended for you to live a lifestyle that only took care of your needs. He wants you to have more than enough to meet your own needs and then to have plenty left over to meet the needs of others (II Corinthians 9). Remember, "God is able to bless you abundantly, so that in all things at all times, having all that you need, you will abound in every good work" (2 Corinthians 9:8).

78

OPERATING IN THE GIFT OF GRACE

By increasing your faith to be a Psalm 112 Man or Woman, you are actually believing God to increase your ability to be a philanthropist. The Apostle Paul calls this the "grace of giving" in 2 Corinthians 8, and he encouraged the people of Corinth to excel in this grace.

By allowing Psalm 112 to come alive in our lives, we excel in this grace of giving. There is a supernatural joy that comes as a result of grace giving. The grace of God is an empowering force that takes giving to a whole new level.

Giving under the anointing and by the grace of God breaks the chains of bondage and brings supernatural provision into people's lives. This kind of giving results in much fruit and thanksgiving to God (2 Corinthians 9:12). It is not giving under compulsion or with any expectation of getting something in return from the receiver. It comes from the very heart of God and demonstrates the amazing and matchless love that He has toward the recipient.

I encourage you to become a carrier of God's love through your giving. Make it your aim to be a Psalm 112 Man or Woman.

"Thanks be to God for his indescribable gift!" (2 Corinthians 9:15)

ABOUT THE AUTHOR

Rick Eaton grew up in Huntington, West Virginia, and was a member and regular church attender at his family's Methodist church along with his father, mother, and two older twin sisters. He received Jesus while a sophomore in High School through the testimony of his wife Robin, who at the time was his high school sweetheart. He graduated from Marshall University in 1978, one week before he and Robin married. The couple's life journey has included living in West Virginia, Pennsylvania, South Florida, Louisiana, and now Mississippi, where they have made their home in the Jackson area since 1988.

Rick and Robin have been married for 41 years. They have two sons ages 37 and 29, two daughters-in-law, and four grandsons ages 13, 10, and 3, and a new-born. Rick and Robin are members of Word of Life Church in Flowood, Mississippi.

Since graduating from college, Rick has worked in several not-for-profit Christian organizations, and owned his own CPA firm from 1988 – 2000. At that time, he sold his accounting practice and became a shareholder in the insurance business owned by his brother-in-law, David White, and John Morgan.

Rick is a shareholder and Chief Operating Officer of AmFirst Holdings, Morgan White Group, and several other related companies headquartered in Ridgeland, Mississippi.

David and Rick, along with their wives, Lynn and Robin, created Wheaton Foundation through which much of their charitable giving is done. Today, their children and their spouses are involved in the management of the foundation as the next generation prepares to take the reins.

CPSIA information can be obtained
at www.ICGtesting.com
Printed in the USA
FSHW021352021120

9 781640 886902